Retrain Your Anxious Brain

How to End Anxiety and Stop Worrying Improving Your Self-Esteem.

Calm Your Mind, Relief Stress and Eliminate Negative Thoughts with Easy Exercises and Guided Meditations

Gabriel Joseph Lawrence

© Copyright 2020 **Gabriel Joseph Lawrence** All Rights Reserved.

This document is aimed to provide accurate and reliable information in the light of the selected topic and all covered issues. This book is sold with the idea that the publisher is not required to render an officially permitted, accounting, or otherwise, qualified services. If advice is required in any way, professional or legal, seasoned experts of the profession should be consulted. According to the Declaration of Principles, accepted and approved by the Committee of Publishers and Associations and Committee of the American Bar Association. It is no way legal to duplicate, transmit or reproduce, any portion of this document in either printed or electronic form. Any recording of this publication is strictly restricted, and the storage of this document is also prohibited unless written permission is offered by the publisher. All rights reserved.

Every information given herein is claimed to be consistent and truthful, in case of any liability, with regard to inattention or otherwise, by any use or abuse of processes, policies, or directions contained within is solely the responsibility of the recipient reader. Under no conditions will any blame or legal responsibility be held against the publisher for any damages, monetary loss or reparation, due to the information herein.

The information herein is provided entirely for informational purposes, and it is universal. The information is provided without any type of guarantee assurance or a contract.

The trademarks that are used within the document are without any consent, and the publication of the trademark is without the backing of the trademark owner or any support. All brands and trademarks used within this book are to clarify the text only, and they are owned by their owners, not affiliated with this publication.

Respective authors of the publication own all copyrights not held by the publisher

Table of Contents

Chapter 1 Anxiety - It's Just A Ghost in My Mind 6
    Symptoms of anxiety.. 8
    Remedies for anxiety 11
    Types of anxiety disorders.. 13

Chapter 2 Where Does My Anxiety Come From? 16
    Causes of anxiety 17

Chapter 3 My Fears, My Strength 25

Chapter 4 Awaken Positive Emotions by Meditations 34
    Using Meditation to Control Emotions 35
    How Meditation Helps Achieve Positive Emotions 45

Chapter 5 Do Not Try to Control Everything, Or You Will End Up Being Controlled 48

Chapter 6 Relax Your Brain 56
    How Can Breathing Contribute to Stress, Anxiety, And Panic? 59

Chapter 7 Improving Self-Confidence 71
    What Is Self Confidence and Why Is It important? 73
    How Can You Build Self Confidence? 75

Chapter 8 Don't Be Strict with Yourself 80

Chapter 9 Learning about Your Body 90
    Musculoskeletal System 90
    Respiratory System 92
    Anxiety and Health 97
    Gastrointestinal 97
    Nervous System 100

Male Reproductive System 102
　　Female Reproductive System 103
Chapter 10 Achieving Self-Awareness **104**
Chapter 11 Surround Yourself with People Who Make You Feel Good .. **118**
Chapter 12 Never Stop, Be Your Change **130**
Conclusions **142**

Chapter 1
Anxiety - It's Just A Ghost in My Mind

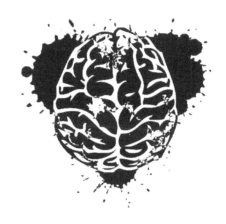

Anxiety is a natural emotion that emerges as a result of stressful situations. It is that overwhelming experience that is between fear and nervousness that kicks in when we are not sure of what the future holds or what is to come in the next few minutes. If you have never experienced a situation that you are about to face, it is just natural that anxiety will kick in. In a scenario where it is your first day at a job interview or even your first day at school, there are good chances of experiencing fear and nervousness to some extent. However, these feelings may not easily dissipate even after the stressful event. So, you may still feel anxious even after the situation which caused the feelings of stress in the first place has passed. Over time, these feelings may even translate to a mental disorder. Anxiety is natural but prolonged anxiety would be a red flag for a mental disorder.

Hence, understanding anxiety and addressing it before it becomes a disorder is essential.

Anxiety is a survival instinct. With anxiety, it shows the alertness of your nervous system and the anticipation of just anything. It shows that the body is ready for whatever is to come out of that bag or door of the unknown. On the verge of a dangerous situation, the body reacts and stimulates the brain to produce the hormone adrenalin. Adrenalin; a neurotransmitter, triggers the response of either facing the situation or running away from it. You either face the situation or take off depending on your experiences and skills. Anxieties, however, revolve around us, may it be at home with family members or at work with your colleagues, it is almost everywhere since its part of life. It may also act as a blind and you may lose an opportunity due to the strike of excessive fear.

Anxiety in kids is also natural and common. Research conducted has concluded that one in every eight children one will experience some kind of anxiety. Children, however, develop ways of coping with anxiety. They obtain the skills and learn from those that are close to them on how to make sure anxiety goes away. They are able to calm themselves from the assistance of the parents, friends, guardians or just anyone involved with them. Nonetheless, the anxiety can continue and become chronic thereby becoming a disorder. Children will show shyness and feelings of isolation while anxious.

Teenagers are mostly anxious. It is normal and natural since they are at a climax point of life. They have the energy and wits; therefore, they face a lot of situations that make them anxious. They have tests, first dates, first job interviews among other things. Since they haven't been exposed to these situations at this point, they are subsequently prone to anxiety. Therefore, it is important for teenagers and young adults to be gradually exposed to such situations.

Symptoms of anxiety

People experience a wide range of symptoms while in an anxious state. People are different and therefore are bound to react differently to different situations or even in similar situations. Some may have an upbringing that made them hardy in that the emotions and anxiety are there but are not as pronounced as in those individuals that had a less traumatic childhood. General anxiety symptoms and signs include the following;

- Increased heart rate is a common symptom in people that are experiencing anxiety. The heart feels like it is in a race and this biologically is a survival tactic. A racing heart will make sure that all your body tissues and organs are alert and ready to react to a potentially dangerous situation. It ensures alertness. It's common, while anxious, to feel your heart beat extremely fast. In case of an encounter with a serious situation, your heart will pump faster to provide the brain and muscles with the energy to fight, or run, as the case may be.

- A period of rapid breathing, it is also a way of getting oxygen to the cells and tissues to ensure energy is available for survival; flight or fight reaction. Some people may even go to the extent of finding a cooling spot just to help relax the breathing rhythm. With the help of a fast-beating heart, oxygen is made available to muscle cells and the brain for a response as is required by the situation at hand.

- Pacing is another symptom that is common. This is also part of restlessness. It feels like your body is not at peace in the surrounding environment. You just feel disturbed and pacing seems to make the edge take off. Restlessness is a telltale sign that a person is nervous. It may even be accompanied by nail biting and other mannerisms. In some cases, folks may not be able to sit still for more a minute.

- Concentration on anything becomes rather difficult; you will feel too troubled to concentrate on any given task. Actually, it becomes a battle to be able to concentrate. It doesn't come automatically because the mind is in stressed and nervous. The mind is so focused on how to maneuver or approach the current situation that it saves a little space to cater to or what is happening at the moment.

- Some individuals will have trouble finding sleep. You might be nervous about an upcoming speech or presentation for example. That night you are likely to be sleepless. Sleep is important since it is the time the mind finds peace and is able to relax and regenerate. Being nervous will get your body alert that sleep will be the last thing on your mind at the time. All there is are chills and thoughts of the unknown that is about to unfold.

- Cold feet, sweaty palms and perhaps tingling arms are also signs of stress. Maybe your boss has summoned you to his office, but you have no idea what this may be about. As such, you are bound to feel tense and may experience the feelings we have mentioned earlier. In fact, "cold feet" is an expression which is commonly used to describe someone who is unsure about doing something.

- Shortness of breath is also another indicator of an anxiety attack. Some individuals can be so nervous that they have trouble breathing. Short breath sometimes escalates to fainting, which is can lead to more complicated health issues.

- Distress or a feeling of anguish is something that you can may not be able to fully explain why it is there or how it came to be. The feeling can be overwhelming and stressful.

- Headaches can also be a symptom of anxiety.

These symptoms, however, can also be experienced as a result of other conditions which aren't necessarily connected to anxiety. Some people will, talk of butterflies in their bellies. This is also a sign of an anxiety attack. Other individuals will experience deeper emotions and symptoms like nightmares, deep memories, painful thoughts and some panic attacks that are out of your control. Fear is also another great indicator of anxiety, maybe fear of a person, a place or perhaps a specific situation. Fear could be the result of prior exposure to traumatic situations or the fear of the unknown.

Remedies for anxiety

However, an anxiety attack is something that can be managed before it reaches the extent of being a serious incident. It is the best when we are able to relax and take control of what is happening around us. To manage these attacks a change in our lifestyle habits may play a huge role. Stress that we cope with daily and anxiety can change with positive habits. Change, however good, is not easy. Healthy living and a positive lifestyle will also keep you a step ahead and in good shape. Some remedies for anxiety attacks include:

- Sleep is very important. It lets your mind reboot and relax. Get enough sleep and let your brain relax so that it can work effectively and achieve its potential.

- Eat healthy foods, keep your body healthy and avoid some unhealthy feeding habits that may have some effects on your body such as your heart. Have a healthy diet every day and lots of fluids.

- Meditating is also a way of strengthening your mind. It is very helpful in controlling anxiety, especially the uncontrolled thoughts and panic attacks.

- Being active through exercise is essential. A healthy body is likely to make it through any anxiety attack. You will recover fast and be in a position to forget the situation and move on.

- Avoid alcohol by all means. It is toxic to your health and body. Alcohol has a way of affecting the brain and by doing so can have an effect on how you perceive things and your reactions.

- Avoid consuming too much caffeine. Caffeine is considered a stimulant, and while it is beneficial is smaller doses, it may have a detrimental effect of your body if consumed in large amounts.

- Smoking is also another habit that is not recommend as part of a healthy lifestyle. Smoking has been proven to lead to any number of health disorders, in particular, lung cancer.

Anxiety is so widespread in that it affects anyone. It can affect adults, teenagers, and even children.

Types of anxiety disorders

Anxiety can be a disorder if not treated early on. These mental disorders of anxiety include;

- **Phobia**. The excessive fear of something specific like heights, swimming among others. It could be a situation, object or activity. Once faced with your phobia, you get in a state of anxiety and fear within you. The fear may be extensive in that it will make even ordinary things seem nearly impossible to you.

- **Panic disorder**. It comes with recurrent panic attacks. You will feel overwhelmed with disabling anxiety and worry. It only gets stronger with the fear of the next panic attack. People with this disorder are always in fear of another instance of a panic attack. It is best if they stop thinking about it and keep the mind busy elsewhere. By finding positive activities, sufferers of panic disorder can find some solace for their symptoms.

- **Social anxiety disorder.** This is the fear of being under people's prejudice. You are constantly fearing people judging and is most prevalent in teenagers. It is mostly fear while in social situations; that's when the anxiety strikes. Anxiety will strike especially when you feel embarrassed or ridiculed; being in those circumstances will raise the level of anxiety.

- **Post-traumatic stress disorder.** The anxiety that comes after a traumatic event. Once you have this disorder, anxiety strikes when there is a part of the situation that appears and has a close link or resemblance to whatever was in the traumatic event. The fear arises with the remembrance of the event or something that resembles the situation.

- **Hypochondria.** It is anxiety that is focused on your health. The individual is constantly in fear of either gaining weight, getting sick, or being afflicted by some illness. Their fear is mainly focused on the wellness of the body. And while fitness matters, a slight discomfort may set off feelings of anxiety about the possibility of having contracted some kind of disease.

- **Separation anxiety disorder.** It is the excessive fear of being alone and away from home or the loved ones. Distress strikes once the person is away from those that mean a lot to him or her. It grows big with time as the more the person is away, the more the anxiety. Some may recover or find ways of reaching out.

- **Obsessive-compulsive disorder.** This condition usually stems from a singular event which lead the sufferer to relive the incident over and over again. In order to cope with their feelings, they develop behaviors and mannerisms that they become obsessed with. For example, excessive hand washing or being overly superstitious can be considered as a part of this condition.

- **General anxiety disorder.** It's a disorder that arises with excessive and unrealistic tension. Tension can be there with no reason or a little disrupted and confused reason. In short, general anxiety disorder may simply stem from prolonged exposure to stress.

Chapter 2
Where Does My Anxiety Come From?

Anxiety may be a natural response in humans but what causes it is not always natural. Researchers believe that it is caused by the combination of two factors, environmental and biological. Anxiety disorder is not a disease that you can be easily diagnosed. It can be a disorder by itself or the result of another associated condition. The influence of substance abuse or the use of medication, among other mental disorders, can also be a cause of anxiety attacks. In this chapter, we will be digging deeper into the causes of anxiety. And while there is a myriad of factors which can cause anxiety, two stand out as the most influential.

Causes of anxiety

Environmental factors

Stress is a normal occurrence in everyday life especially for those in stressful environments. Nevertheless, if the stress is prolonged and overlooked it can be a source of even more than anxiety. Long term toxic relationships or being in a place you have always disliked for a long time can lead to the development of anxiety.

Those people that battle with stress are prone to struggle with anxiety, too. Stress may stem from work, a relationship such as marriage, financial difficulties among others. They will contribute to the emergence of the anxiety attack which may progress to anxiety disorder if no control measures are put in place. Stress is capable of weakening the part of the brain that is responsible for combating stress itself. Not only can it affect that but also the brain's neurotransmitters. It is believed to affect the production of these neurotransmitters and hormones responsible for maintaining the wellness of the brain. The mind will, therefore, become overwhelmed and lack the power to fight anxiety as it used to. As weak as it becomes it means that the individual will be shaken even by the mild instances of stress since the stress-fighting mechanism is so weak to protect against the attack.

Our life depends so much on the millions of experiences that help us understand life and eventually see the circumstances of life from different angles. Our upbringing has a lot to do with the way we see life. It determines our personality and also plays a key role in the development of anxiety. We react in much the same ways that we saw our parents while growing up. Having overprotective parents or limited social interaction while growing up may lead to social anxiety. If your parents are overly concerned about a situation, they may inadvertently instill a fear in your mind. Fear can also grow as a result of abuse and bullying during childhood.

Indeed, the experiences lived during childhood play a pivotal role in shaping our personality and the way that we react to the world around us as adults. That is why childhood traumas tend to be the leading cause of anxiety in adults.

Trauma can be seen as a life-altering situation that remains engraved in the mind of an individual. Severe trauma includes situations which can be horrendous, violent or even life-threatening experiences. Post-traumatic stress disorder (PTSD) is a result of traumatic experiences which go unresolved. Nonetheless, kids find it easier to cope with the trauma, and recover from it, as they join adulthood. Although, the scars may still be there, and the anxiety may still be persistent. With trauma, an environment that has a close resemblance to that scene of trauma or any linkages to the same has the potential of causing an anxiety attack. Their anxiety handling system is altered in that they no longer process extreme cases of stress or low-stress levels as they did process before the trauma.

Change is good but has its own challenges. Change has been put forward also as a contributor to anxiety. It is true we feel unsafe in new places, though some people are able to adapt faster while some of us take longer to make adjustments to change. New environments put stress on us with emotions that may be unfamiliar. Anxiety develops from this uneasiness. Change however is not only environmental but also emotional, like the loss of a person you were so close to. Significant changes can grow out of proportion is they are not addressed in time. They may lead to full-blown anxiety disorders.

It is important to keep in mind that catching traumatic events early on can lead to a healthy recovery. For instance, if you have been in a car accident, you may have recollections, flashbacks and memories of this distressing event. As a result, you may find yourself suffering from the long-term events of such a situation unless you are able to do something about it early on. If so, then the chances you have for a full recovery are far greater than if you simply let such feelings fester over time. Ultimately, your ability to deal with issues early on will enable you to find the right way of addressing them before they become a serious psychological condition.

Did you know that being afraid of being anxious will also make you even more anxious? In panic attacks, individuals are in constant fear of when the panic attacks will strike again. That constant fear keeps them very anxious. Why should we fear being anxious? The anxiety now becomes a vicious cycle. It is not only in people with panic attacks, but normal people may also experience this. Maybe there is an activity that you did some time ago and made you feel chills and when the activity is brought to you again the chills resurface. You fear to get chills again as a result of that first encounter. For instance, if have an unpleasant experience while riding a motorbike ride, it means that in future you may never try it again. The mere thought of this situation is enough to cause anxiety. Some are afraid that the severity of anxiety they felt at the time may strike again at the sight of the object that makes them. That constant fear is what fuels anxiety thereby creating the vicious cycle.

Healthy living and positive lifestyle habits will help cope with stress. Exercise and good living habits will keep every organ in your body healthy and in good working condition. When we practice poor lifestyle habits, we become prone to getting anxiety attacks. The brain and body will produce fewer neurotransmitters and hormones capable of coping with stress which makes you vulnerable and weak in warding off an anxiety attack.

Genetics

It is generally believed that anxiety disorder can be hereditary. In some cases, children may inherit overly nervous and anxious emotions from one or both parents. Research is still ongoing to identify if genetics are truly behind all this excessive expression of fear and anxiety. It has however been proven that anxiety disorder can be passed down to the next generation as a result of upbringing and conditioning more than genetics.

As such, upbringing also has a link to genetics; some children will obtain anxiety attacks or disorders after much interaction with their parents or being close to them. The brain capacity and how it works can be linked to heredity, therefore, the coping capacity to stress can be inherited making the anxiety disorder a gene-related condition. There are some pieces of evidence that were put forward and they showed anxiety disorders run in families.

Studies have also shown that some individuals have a great tendency for getting anxiety disorder compared to other just because of their physical makeup. Therefore, it can be inferred that in some cases, there are underlying physiological conditions which cause anxiety such as lesions in specific parts of the brain. These lesions may inhibit an individual's ability to deal with stress and anxiety in a natural manner.

Medical factors

However small the percentage of diseases that are capable of causing an anxiety attack, they do exist. These conditions will further the anxiety condition since they disrupt brain functionality hence affecting how the brain reacts to stress factors. Neurotransmitter and hormone production may be affected as well. The brain is a critical organ and an attack on it may bring about significant harm. Nonetheless, there may be no evidence of a physical condition. Still, the symptoms persist in such a way that the sufferer shows all signs without there being a clear physiological cause. Under such circumstances, the causes of anxiety may be related to a purely emotional cause or another undetected physical condition.

Biologically, the human body is wired to cope with any situation that arises. The thyroid gland is a body part that produces hormones which help deal with stress. These hormones are released to the bloodstream and are useful in controlling body metabolism and energy levels. Thyroid glands contribute to anxiety if there is more production of the hormone than necessary. Too much thyroid hormone in your body will bring about anxiety symptoms like sleeplessness, rapid breathing, fast-beating heart, the nervousness among others. It is important to have the gland checked if you feel more anxious especially while faced by a situation and the anxiety does not calm down even after the exit of the stimulus.

Medical conditions like hypertension, cancer, hormonal imbalances, among others, can also produce anxiety as one of its effects. In the case of cancer patients, anxiety can become severe due to the stress of the uncertainty surrounding the illness itself and its corresponding treatment. But not only cancer patients can be prone to anxiety. Anyone who is going through a serious illness may have to deal with severe anxiety, as well. A serious condition can lead to constant fear and nervousness.

Allergies can also contribute to anxiety. For instance, if you suffer from food allergies, you may feel anxious about your diet. You may not feel totally safe when consuming food, especially if you haven't prepared it yourself, since there may be traces of the element which may cause a severe allergic reaction.

Alteration in brain chemistry

Imbalance in the normalcy of the brain's chemicals has been linked to anxiety attacks. The individuals suffering from anxiety disorders are likely to have some problems with their brain chemistry. Hormone and neurotransmitter production may be faulty. Neurotransmitters include serotonin, norepinephrine and gamma-aminobutyric acid (GABA). Nevertheless, research is yet to determine if chemical imbalances cause anxiety, or the other way around. Through therapy, be it through medication or some other drug-free treatment, most individuals are able to regain their proper flow and production of neurotransmitters.

Brain imaging devices have shown a discovery that those with anxiety disorders have more brain activity compared to those who don't. In general, anxiety keeps most of the brain active for a longer period of time. This explains the high levels of fatigue that arise as a result of anxiety. Anxiety disorders linked to brain functionality may occur due to anomalies in the blood flow in the brain or metabolism. These changes, however, have been proven to be temporary. Therefore, under treatment one can regain the power to cope with stress.

Anxiety is treatable regardless of your circumstances or upbringing. All you need to do is try and understand where it comes from and why. Once you establish the source of your anxiety, the path to recovery becomes a lot clearer. The hardest part of anxiety is to pinpoint the exact cause of the feeling. It requires internalizing and spending some time with yourself to establish what makes you so nervous since mild anxiety here and there is part of life. What is not normal is anxiety that never subsides or dies a natural death after the exit of the stimulus.

Chapter 3
My Fears, My Strength

Most times, people experience fear both knowingly and unknowingly. However, it's almost impossible for people to define fear because it comes out strong as an emotion that seems indefinable. Fear is an uncomfortable emotion brought by a person's notion that someone or something is likely to be a threat or painful. When a person is always uncomfortable around someone or something, they are afraid of both. Fear is sometimes good because it keeps a person from danger by alerting someone not to do something. However, most times, fear is terrible, especially when it prevents someone from taking risks and enjoying life. Fear often keeps a person away from self-realization and growth while reducing the potential of discovering personal strength.

Without your power, not only do you stop taking risks, but you also stop dreaming of being big. Fear keeps you away from dreaming, and without dreams, you become hopeless and resentful. Sometimes fear is forced upon us, maybe as kids growing up, or by people surrounding us. Most times, however, fear begins from the mind when you start doubting, your self-worth. This kind that starts from the brain will steal your joy and keep you away from everything that could have made you happy. It keeps you away from the working risks and even relationship risks.

At work, one will be afraid to ask for a greater challenge. Also, when they know they deserve a promotion, they will not ask for it. A fearful person will consider others more deserving than themselves always, not because it's the truth, but because they are afraid to fight for themselves. Fears are very controlling; you might know what you need to do, but your fear will direct you to do something different. Fear will control your emotions so that not only are you afraid, but you are also experiencing other negative emotions.

Fear comes in various forms for different people. For some its anxiety, feeling nervous, feeling confused, and feeling unmotivated. Fear sometimes is uncertain; you feel that you are going through something, but you can't precisely identify what it actually is. But when you feel unhappy, and you have nothing to look forward to, chances are you are going through a specific type of fear, and all you need is to identify the source of that fear.

Everyone goes through fear; what makes us different is our ability to identify and face it. Fear can be turned into personal strength. All one needs to do, instead of running and hiding from it, is to face it.

Here are some strategies that can help you turn fear into personal strength.

- **Self-reflection.** Go through a self-reflection journey and find out what the fear is. You cannot deal with something you have not identified. Get to know what the fear is so that you know where it comes from. What provokes the fear and the feelings that bring fear are very important to identify. This is what will help you have the strength to go for the fear. Engaging in self-reflection means that you are ready to get to know the roots of your fear. It might not be a pleasant journey, but it will certainly be a worthwhile one. It is looking at what could possibly go wrong if you faced the fear and what could happen if you didn't face the fear. Sometimes, to identify the fear, you need to look at it from a third-person perspective. Due to emotions that tie us to the fear, recognizing it from a personal perspective is usually tricky, and that's why the third persona is important. Here is where you need to be honest with yourself by identifying the harsh reality you are living. With introspection, folks often find that fear is derived from negative self-talk from within oneself. For example, you might be compelled apply for a promotion at work but then talk yourself out of it because you tell yourself that others are more deserving than you.

When you identify the source of fear, it is now time to start the positive self-talk. This is the best inspiration you will ever need. Start telling yourself that you are the best there is, believe in yourself and talk yourself into it. Tell yourself that you are more than what you are afraid of and that fear will not define you as a person. Engaging in positive self-talk will help you deal with your worries so that they will neither control you nor put you away from accomplishing your personal ambitions. Self-talk may seem very petty, but it goes a long way. The more you have positive talks within yourself, the more you believe in yourself and the less afraid you become. The best way to practice positive self-talk is by standing in front of the mirror and addressing yourself.

- **Assess your fear.** This means that you get to look at your fears more deeply. What does the fear prevent you from doing? What does it make you do? Remember that fear is not always bad; if it helps you keep away from trouble, then it should be embraced. It does not make you weak when you adopt some form of fear if it's doing you well because that's a reasonable fear. However, if the fear keeps you away from all the good things in life, then you need to assess it. Find out the worst that could happen if you faced your fear. Are you afraid that your work presentation will not go well? As such, is this the cause of your fear? Search within yourself to find out the worst that you could happen if you went ahead and presented it anyway. If you think others will laugh at you, be courageous and trust that you will do your best during the presentation. Assessing also means that you look at your fear and ask yourself what will happen if you don't face it at all. You could choose to avoid the fear by not dealing with it, but you should ask yourself about the consequences of choosing not to. If you wanted to start your own business but choose not to because you think you are not good enough or not ready, ask yourself what the result would be. This could encourage you quite a bit because you realize that facing the fear outdoes ignoring it. It will take so much courage for you to face your fear, but once you do, you will wonder what was making you so afraid. So, in the end, it counts so much when you can confidently face your fear.

- **Action time**. You have already weighed your options and assessed all the possible outcomes for facing and ignoring your fears. You can tell what the right thing to do for your fear is, whether embracing if it's the right kind of dealing with it or if it's not. Act by doing what you think should be done because waiting will only damage you further. Don't pressure yourself, take each step at a time in the beginning. Of course, the first step will always be the hardest to take. It will take time and a lot of downfalls to finally feel that you have done well to overcome the fear. The most important thing to do is to remember not to give up when you find yourself falling along the way, so don't be discouraged.

- **Acknowledge yourself**. Celebrate yourself for all the fears you are able to overcome. You deserve to acknowledge your achievements. There is no big or small fear; any could be damaging enough. The fact that you were able to overcome it means a lot. Don't overlook your success in fighting the fear because this will be an excellent motivation for you in that you can overcome anything. Each time you celebrate your success in overcoming worry, you remind yourself that there is nothing you cannot face. For others, it may seem irrelevant, but you know what the fear was doing to you and how much more damaged it would have left you had you done nothing about it.

- **Rise above your fears**. You have already identified your fear, you have dealt with it and have celebrated your triumph it. You need to rise up from the fear. Don't keep remembering the fear because the more you remember it, the more likely it is to give you negative emotions. Negative emotions will pull back to the fear slowly without your realization. You, therefore, need to let go of it completely; let it go because if you continue holding on to it, you continue to widen the possibility of its recurring. Rising up means that you forget all the negatives and start focusing on the positive things ahead. Start focusing on what you can do to avoid any more possibility of this kind of fear. Build yourself by going for everything that fears stop you from going for. Go for everything that you could never have gone for had you not faced the fear. In doing this, a person can now be sure that they are finally over their fear.

Changing Fear into Strength

Turning fear into strength means that you do exactly what your negative fears tell you not to do. You may be afraid that people think you are weak; the best way to overcome this is by working on yourself. This could be by believing more in yourself than you currently do, and it could also mean that you need to do something for yourself that will stop others from seeing you as weak. When you are afraid of other's opinions of you because it makes you feel bad, start appreciating what they have to say. You can start by telling yourself that their opinion about you will help you change some things you could never have noticed about yourself. When you are so afraid of being heartbroken, ask yourself why you are so scared. It could be that you are afraid of being alone. The right thing to do would be to actually take a break from the relationship. Maybe you are afraid of being alone, and that is why a possible heartbreak breaks you. When you take a break, you may realize that it is not as bad as you think it is and you can grow more on yourself in readiness for anything. When you are afraid of failure because you think it will determine you as a person, start defining yourself. Identify yourself worth and find out what you as a person.

When you are sure that you are more than your failures, you will start to appreciate yourself more and therefore, will not be afraid to take risks. If you are worried that you are the reason why others are not doing well because you are pulling them behind, start working on yourself and see how best you can work as a group. Start finding your unique factor that will help the group and one that will make you more productive in the group. When you are scared that you will be blamed for any losses in the business, start working towards being better so that you will always be accountable for all your actions. The thing is when you start turning your fear into strength, you start achieving more than could ever have been possible.

Your fear is often your strength and that is why it can be frightening to use it. People are even afraid of success; some people are so scared of being wealthy because it makes them a potential target of attack from others. Some people are so afraid of taking medical tests because they feel they are better off not finding out that they are sick. They think they are ill and so for them taking the analysis seems to be frightening for them. It would be easier if they took the test because then it will mean an earlier treatment before the illness becomes too severe. But also, the test may come out negative and may mean that the person can now take preventive measures. Fear is not something to keep away from; it is something to face. That which you are most afraid of is what could potentially make you greater than you could have ever imagined.

Chapter 4
Awaken Positive Emotions by Meditations

As human beings, we are often faced by situations that make us want to do something that will cool our negative emotions. You could be so angry that you feel the only way you could calm yourself down is by screaming or throwing a tantrum. You feel like that is the best reaction at that time, but the truth is reacting towards a negative emotion is short-term. It will only cool you for a while, but eventually, you need something to help you get rid of the emotions altogether. Your emotions will continue to control you as long as you continue to react to them instead of finding a permanent solution for them.

Managing your negative emotions is not about hiding or denying them. Denying what you feel will not take them away from you; it will not turn the negative emotions into positive ones. The best way to turn negative emotions without acting irrationally whenever provoked to do so is by practicing meditation. What meditation does is to help a person gain control over their emotions so that the individual learns to manage their emotions before they become uncontrollable outbursts.

Using Meditation to Control Emotions

- **Find a center of focus**. Being human means that you are constantly faced with a barrage of thoughts at any given moment. Your emotions originate from your thoughts, and that is why your emotions keep changing. At one point, you might be feeling happy, the next you are sad, and the next minute you might have a different feeling that you can't explain where it came from. All this is because of the various thoughts that keeping running through your mind. You will feel what your mind is thinking and therefore, the only way to control your feelings is controlling your brain, which isn't very practical to do. However, you can regulate your feelings by ensuring that your mind is calm. When your mind is thinking about different things; your emotions will change alongside it. But when you are only thinking about a specific thing, then your emotions are calmly regulated. The way to calm your mind is settling your mind on a single point and meditating over that point. Whenever you feel like you are wandering off in your thoughts, fight hard to bring back your mind to the point of focus. Practicing this will make your mind calm and collected. You become more aware of your present, and you can focus on your current emotions. It won't be easy to find the focus at first, so you need to keep practicing because you are exercising the brain to center its focus. You are simply doing a mental exercise to train your mind to stay in one place and therefore focusing on one emotion at a time. Take deep breaths, breathing in and out, and try to get your mind at your center of focus. Whenever you are wandering in thought, take deep breaths and amidst that gather your mind back to where you want to focus.

- **Be self-compassionate**. Being empathetic with yourself is very important. It means that you are fully aware of yourself in terms of your thoughts and emotions. When you are aware of this, you, therefore, understand that your emotions are not unique; everyone goes through the same emotions. You accept that your emotions as being human and therefore are not too harsh on yourself. You, therefore, are able to treat yourself with kindness whenever you experience emotions that you do not like. This means, that whenever you experience negative emotions, you do not let them break you down. A few simple steps can guide the way to self-compassion:

- First, recognize your thoughts. You could think of how much you dislike a person, and the emotion that follows this thought. Usually, a thought will be accompanied by an emotion that backs up the thought. So, this is where you get to identify both the thoughts and the feelings that follow in concert.

- Next, when you have in mind what your thoughts and emotions are, you therefore need to realize that you are not the only one going through it. Keep in mind that whatever your thoughts and emotions are, other people in your situation would have felt the same. Do not be shy or ashamed of accepting this fact because this is where you get to practice self-compassion.

- Finally, you need to act kindly towards yourself. By encouraging yourself either in thoughts or actions. You can tell yourself that your thought will change if you want to tune it. Or you can be kind by choosing a positive action instead of the negative action your brain is telling you to.

- **Meditating on self-compassion is very important**. It means that you are going to deal with your emotions with self-compassion. By being empathetic with yourself, you will turn your negative emotions into positive ones. When you breathe, as you inhale, you need to think of yourself with self-compassion and welcome all the positivity that comes along with it. As you exhale, you should let out all the negative emotions inside of you. Meditating on self-compassion will turn your negative emotions into positive ones. You will find more reason to be kind to yourself; that is the most significant source of positive emotions. When you are kind to yourself, you do not pursue suffering since you know that negative emotions cause a great deal of stress. When you want to be kind to yourself, it means you want to happy and therefore you will encourage positive emotions that lead happiness. By meditating on self-compassion, you will encourage yourself to take more risks because you know that risks expand your growth. With self-compassion, you give yourself positive emotions that no matter what happens after the risks, you will still be happy. As a person with self-compassion, you will encourage yourself to understand that failures will not reduce you into nothingness. Meditating on self-compassion, therefore, is what will give you the courage and strength to promote positive emotions for yourself.

- **Putting your personal situation into perspective**. Sometimes, we exaggerate our emotions or make them seem such a big deal as though the world revolves around us. Taking time to zoom out means that you look at yourself as the simplest thing that exists in the universe. This thought pattern helps put you into perspective within the universe itself. Meditate on how big the world is and how many people there are in the world who are going through the same thing as you. Meditating on how you fit within the grander scheme of things in the world. This will help you see that you have a place in this world just like everyone else. You will feel stronger to face whatever it is that was holding you down; you will think that you can do it because you and your situation are very not that different from what others are also going through. Sometimes you feel so angry that you think you can explode and even taken down the world with you because of how angry you are. When you zoom out and meditate about that which makes you so upset, you might see that you were probably blowing things out of proportion. You will even be able to see the positive ways of handling it, dealing with it will be more exciting to you. This is because you meditated and found out that there is no greater thing than being positively minded. Positive emotions will be awakened because you will realize how many greater problems there are in the world and how many people are going through worse experiences than yourself. This kind of meditation not only shifts your emotions, but it also tunes your mind into calmness, and therefore all your thoughts will be positive moving forward. Positive thoughts equal positive emotions.

- **Visualizing the emotions you want**. This means that you imagine positive emotions even before they happen. When you know you are about to go through something difficult, visualize a positive emotion that you will want to feel when that time comes. You can also imagine offering positive emotions to others so that you are able to prepare yourself in advance. This exercise can be centered in three different perspectives based on the possible encounters which you may have during a regular day. When you visualize yourself reacting to each situation with positive emotions, you then become ready to offer them the same once you are in contact with them. The following tips will help your meditation so that when you meet these three people, you are able to be kind to them and express positive emotions.

- **Meditation for relationships**. Meditate on a close friend you want to express positive emotions towards. The easiest way to bring such a person in your mind is through visualization. This technique will help calm your mind from thinking of other people other than the one you want to focus on. After you have the person in your mind, visualize them close to you, either sitting or standing next to you. Acknowledge how their presence feels to you. Think about what this person makes you feel. Try to hold on to that feeling for a little while. When you identify the first feeling this person brings you, try your best to acknowledge their feelings. Acknowledge that this person has gone through both positive and negative emotions like fear and sadness, or joy and happiness. Next, focus on how much you want to brighten up their lives. Whether they are struggling or whether they are flying high, you want to be a positive influence on them. In your mind, where the meditation is taking place, imagine yourself being helpful to that person especially if they are going through a rough time.

- **Focus on a stranger**. Put aside the image of your friend, and imagine a stranger, a person you have just met recently and do not know anything about. In essence, think about someone that you do not know as well as you do a close friend. At this point, it is useful to visualize how the presence of this stranger makes you feel. Acknowledge their struggles as well how they may be trying to connect to you. As a matter of fact, you might even seem unapproachable. Also, identify other emotions this person may be going through like happiness, satisfaction or even stress. Try to focus on any other challenges you think they might be going through. Then in your meditative state, imagine yourself being kind to them. Imagine yourself being the shoulder they need to lean on. Calm them and be helpful to them as if they were there with you.

- **Focusing on a threat**. Bring into imagination someone you feel always brings the worst in you. Someone that you think has the power to always bring out your negative emotions of fear, frustration, anger, and resentment. Observe how their presence makes you feel and focus on it for a while. Sometimes the feeling is so unpleasant that you want to avoid this experience altogether. But it is good to identify such feelings despite how they make you feel. Acknowledge that, like you, this person is human and has flaws. You feel afraid, but so do they because no matter how uncomfortable you feel about them, they may also feel the same about you. Identify all the feelings you might be potentially going through; the very person who makes you feel threatened might also be going through the same when thinking about you. Acknowledge that this person could be posing as a threat to you because they need some kindness from someone and are not receiving it. Accept that, just like you, this person also has someone who they feel threatens them. As you meditate, imagine yourself being kind to that person. Visualize in your mind awakening the positive emotions within you and sharing with this other person. Give them the assurance that everything will be okay, be kind to them and express your warmth, kindness, and affection towards them.

Finally, meditate by visualizing all three people around you. In reality, these three may seem very different with very different reactions toward you. However, in your mind, you need to make these three become one. Identify that the all three go through the same emotions and that it only takes you to change your perception about them. In your mind, give the three of them assurances as if they were one, they would feel loved.

Often, we are unable to overcome negative emotions because, amidst our challenges, we forget that nothing is permanent. We experience too much hurt and pain that we think that there is no way we'll be able to overcome the situation. One of the greatest ways to awaken positive emotions is by keeping in mind that nothing is permanent. No matter how challenging we think of our situations are, we need to meditate on how impermanent they are. Meditating on how it will all soon the end will help ease the situation.

Here is a simple procedure of how to go about this:

Imagine the situation you are going through and how it can be broken down into the smallest unit of time possible. You can break the timing down into seconds, minutes and hours. Sometimes when you say four weeks, it sounds much more than when you call it one month. But this is different for each person. Therefore, thinking of the situation in the time frame your mind feels is the least will help you realize that it is not as long as you might have thought. While meditating, it is good to keep repeating in your mind that it too will pass. Remind yourself of all the difficulties you went through in the past that you never thought would pass. Meditate on that time when you felt that there was no end in sight, yet you manage to pull through and see things to the end.

Think about how much time it took to overcome that thought and remind yourself that you could overcome this also within such a time frame or even quicker. This will awaken your positive emotions as you begin to feel that there is nothing you cannot handle. Your positive emotions need motivation, and this motivation is the thought based on the fact that negative situations can't last as long as you fear. By undertaking this meditation where you remind yourself that nothing will last, you excite your positive emotions, and they become more active than any other emotions inside you.

Meditating helps relieve the damaging emotions that interfere with one's wellbeing, both physically and mentally. Emotions like anxiety, depression, and stress can be addressed in this manner. Meditation also is attributed to giving someone a strong sense of belief in themselves. This is the hallmark of someone who is positively minded. Meditation is also the greatest way to get rid of negative emotions and embrace positive emotions that make a person find happiness and the thrill of life. Some common meditation techniques work so much better and quickly bring a person to more positive emotions. Most people don't understand how this is possible so below is a brief description of how it works.

How Meditation Helps Achieve Positive Emotions

- **Calming the mind**. Meditation helps calm the mind. It allows the mind some silence. This is the only time the mind takes a break. It is important to give the mind this break because the more overworked your mind gets, the more likely you are to experience negative emotions. All emotions are processed by the mind. So, positive emotions will certainly have a calming effect. You cannot provoke positive emotions when your mind is exhausted. The first emotion that the brain will throw you in such a state is stress. However, if you want your emotions to be happy ones, you need your mind to be peaceful, and this is what meditation does.

- **Placing yourself in the present**. Meditation helps you forget the past because it is usually the past that gives us negative emotions. When you always remember things from the past, they invoke negative emotions in you, the ones you felt then, yet you feel as though you are experiencing them right now. Meditation helps you let go. When you calm your mind, and take deep breaths, you are able to release the negativity. You then begin to live in the moment enjoying everything as it happens and not even worrying about tomorrow. Dealing with each moment at a time awakens the positive emotions of bravery. These emotions allow you to live in the present without being overly concerned about the past or the future. Positive emotions do not want to be tied down to any worries, and such problems are eliminated when you meditate and place yourself in the present.

- **Modification of the conscious.** Through continued meditation, you bring your mind to a state where only positive thoughts are felt. Positive thoughts are the source of positive emotions; the two go hand in hand. It is impossible to have positive thoughts and have negative emotions, while it is also possible to have negative thoughts and have positive emotions. Therefore, this means that having positive thoughts is the best way to lead into positive emotions. What meditation does is alter the negative thoughts or control them to a more reasonable level. You will find that when you continue practicing meditation, you start to think more positively, and when your emotions become more positive with time.

Meditation has the power of taking the mind in a happier place where you get to experience all the desired emotions.

Meditation usually happens in two ways which are either by concentrating or non-concentrating forms. Concentrating involves focusing on something other than yourself, like an object, while the non-concentrating consists of a person searching deeper within yourself. This could be by focusing on breathing, thoughts, and feelings. It is possible for one meditation to involve both forms; it all boils down to a person's strength to go deeper into meditation. What is most important, however, is that as you meditate, you internalize everything so profoundly that moving forward, it becomes easier to deal with your emotions. When you achieve positive emotions after meditation, do not stop at that, make it a habit so that eventually, the positive emotions and thoughts become part of you.

Chapter 5
Do Not Try to Control Everything, Or You Will End Up Being Controlled

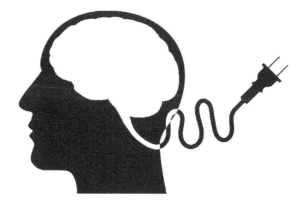

All humans have exceptional abilities. We all have different capabilities but trying to control everything will only lead you to trouble. When you try to control everything, you will end up being controlled. It is impossible to control everything at once; you must leave room for what you can't control. Letting your feelings control what you do is the riskiest thing you can ever do to yourself. Be the one to control what you think and what you do. This is why it is important to focus on your thoughts, and thereby your feelings, so that they don't get the best of you.

Many people, especially leaders of various groups, always try to control everything that happens around them. This is called micromanaging. For example, you find someone is a treasurer in a group. So, they want to play the role of the chairperson, the secretary and the chief of staff at the same time. This person will end up losing themselves because they won't get the chance to handle all these duties quite as well as they though. As a result, they start to panic and are left thinking how well they could have done everything.

Another example is where someone is in the struggling to become financially independent. They will try doing everything that they think can earn them money. If their endeavors don't work out, they begin to worry about their options, thinking of what they will do next if those fail, too. These people allow themselves to be controlled by the lust of money to the point where their mind can't settle down because they are in the hunt for money. If they just calm down and stick to one thing that they can easily handle, they can earn themselves a decent income. That way they cannot be overpowered by the fear of not having enough. And while they may still be concerned with missed opportunities, at least they will feel comfortable with the living they have made for themselves.

Now, take a look at yourself at a personal level. What is it that leads you to be anxious? Is it an event? Is it your past? Is it the present or the future? Are you in a position to tell the main cause of your anxiety? If so, are you ready to take a step away from it? It is not easy to rub off something you had once started and let it go off your mind completely. However, it is very important for a person to identify what is causing unnecessary fear and worry in them that can be dangerous to their mental health and find a way of overcoming it for them to remain free from anxiety.

Anything can cause trouble in our mind and change how we operate in one form or another. It even changes how we respond to different things and can also reduce our performance in various activities. It is not always easy to realize this until it goes deep to an extent that you find yourself trying to fight some fears that we never there before, or that were present, but you could not notice because they had not become that severe.

You can fall victim to an event that will leave you restless and thinking "what's next?" You can be left to think about the "what ifs", or what could you have done to stop it from happening. The feeling that is imposed on you by an event is what will drive so many questions in your mind to a point that you won't be able to answer. This is what will lead to you being anxious.

The fact of the matter is that most people can only speculate about the "what ifs" of life. You can speculate all you want about how life would have been different had things worked out in a different manner. However, this is a dangerous game as speculating about the past may only lead to opening wounds that are still way too fresh.

In this regard, it is worth making sense of why things happened they way they did and understanding your thought process when they did. After all, the old saying "it seemed like a good idea at the time" actually rings true more often than not. When you realize that many of the decisions that you made hinged upon the information available at the time, then you can begin to avoid beating yourself up about them.

Of course, it is also true that "hindsight is 20/20 vision". It is perfectly true that bad decisions could have easily been avoided had you known what you know now. But the fact of the matter is that is practically impossible to have all available information at the time of making a choice. This is especially true when you find out important information after the fact. Ultimately, there is no point in beating yourself up over such circumstances. If you find that you made a mistake, then it is best to attempt to rectify it and move on.

Something that had happened to you in the past can also make you anxious. Think of a bad situation that you went through in the past. Maybe you went through a particularly challenging childhood. Such a life can leave you with indelible marks that may follow you throughout your life. So, when you look back at such events, you may feel anxious. In some cases, you may even enter depression as a result of these unresolved issues.

One thing that is for sure: this is the past and you have no control over the past. You can change the future when you control the present, but you cannot control the past. You have to convince yourself and accept that this is something that was beyond your control. You must first be ready to let go of the situation and focus on what's ahead. If you could control the past, then you could go back and change any circumstances which may have affected you negatively. Unfortunately, this is a power that we do not possess.

The present can cause anxiety as well. When you are not living a good life as others who are close to you, you are tempted to think that you are not as lucky as the other people and that you should not be in the same group as them. You fear interacting with others because of their high standard of living. You start stressing yourself thinking of how hard you can work to be where they are and fit in the same environment and class as them.

You expose yourself to too much pressure of trying to fit in a different kind of environment when you should be focusing on how what is important and what is making you feel alive. You should understand that everyone has a different destiny. You can start from one point but headed to totally different directions. Trying to be where the other person is when that is not what was meant for you is being unfair to yourself. You are allowing yourself to be controlled by the would because you are trying to control your living standards, yet you never worked for it from the start.

You can't control everything in life. The people you are competing with may have inherited this kind of life from their parents while you, on the other hand, perhaps didn't have a parent to set the pace for this kind of life. You have what your parents gave you. Therefore, you have to appreciate and take good care of it rather than trying to force yourself to something that you cannot afford. The struggle you go through trying to be in the same class as your friends are what causes unending stress. You fear to fail because your friends seem to be doing very well while you are not. You let the idea of other people define who you should be.

Another thing that threatens the lives of many people is the fear of the future. They are so concentrated on how tomorrow will be that they forget about the living today. This can lead to missing opportunities at various points in life. Then, when the individual realizes that they overlooked potentially good opportunities because they were focused on the future, they may resort to blaming others for their shortcomings. Indeed, this is the type of trap in which people can get easily sucked into without realizing it.

You can only control the future if you take good care of the present and handle things the right way. Are you going to buy this better future you are talking about or will you fix it on one that has been built from the start? This is something that is that can be very difficult and only causes more stress to the brain than the beauty it adds in a person's heart. So, it is best to be prepared for the future, but not obsessing over what may not even come to pass.

For you to live a better kind of lifestyle, you should allow yourself to identify the source of your instability and work towards making a better ending. Think about what is making you be anxious and let it all slide. Stop holding on to it and let go as you look for a better way of doing what is within your reach to change your destiny. There is no harm in failing, but there is great harm in refusing to set yourself free.

There are several things that can never be controlled by a normal human being. Don't tie yourself up in the attempt of trying to control everything. Just do what you can and avoid what you cannot control. There is someone who is in a position to control what is beyond your control so never try making yourself sweat so hard trying to fix what is beyond your capability. Worrying too much is what causes unnecessary anxiety in many people.

One thing that everyone needs to understand and accept is that we can never do everything alone. We all need each other's support in the struggle of finding ourselves. When we let everything that is stressing us slide, then we are left on the right track to chase success without fear. Sticking to something that you can never change is what impacts fear in us and hinder us from fighting hard towards getting what we have been working for quite some time.

When we try to control everything, we are setting a trap for ourselves. It is so clear that you can't chase two birds at a time because when they take different directions, you won't kill them with one stone. You will have to decide which one to go after or you end up losing both of them. This is the same thing that happens when we try to control everything. We reach a point that we have no choice left but to lose everything even what we deserved.

You should not allow yourself to be a slave of anxiety. Do what you can do and leave what you cannot. If it is a mistake that you had made, accept and move on. No one is perfect and what had already happened cannot be undone so nothing should tie you to it. Other people's opinion of you does not matter anymore. What they think or say can never stop you from moving on. If one idea failed, you still have room to start afresh and make a brighter ending. Say no to worries, say no to anxiety. Let everything take care of itself.

Chapter 6
Relax Your Brain

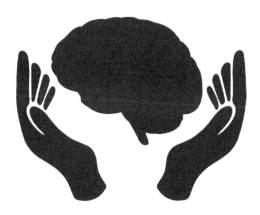

What comes into your mind when you hear the term relaxation? Now, you are probably thinking that relaxation is about flopping on the couch and watching a nice movie or TV program after having a stressful day. But this is not what relaxation is because it does not reduce the damaging effects caused by stress. Relaxation requires you to activate your body's natural relaxation response. Activating your body's natural relaxation response means that you take yourself to a state of deep rest that is capable of putting the brakes on stress, slowing your breathing and heart rate, lowering your blood pressure and bringing your body and mind back into balance. This can be done by practicing and adopting relaxation techniques like deep breathing, yoga, rhythmic exercise, meditation or tai chi.

Well, you may decide to go for some professional acupuncture session or massage, but the fact is that you can do most of the relaxation techniques on your own. Furthermore, technology today is so advanced and cuts across all sectors and therefore you can also choose to use the aid of free downloaded audio or mobile applications to guide you through your meditation. Remember that every individual has their own preferences. Therefore, no single brain relaxation technique works equally well for everyone. Use the technique that you feel resonates with you and that fits your lifestyle. Choose the technique that you feel you can focus your mind on to activate the relaxation response. With this approach, you will have to take your time to try different techniques for you to find the technique that best fits you. Once you do, you can also incorporate regular practice which will help you to reduce everyday stress and anxiety thus you will have improved sleep, boost your moods and energy, and in the end, you will have good health and wellbeing.

Relaxation Technique #1: Deep Breathing

Breathing is a necessity of life. Breathing occurs without much thought. Breathing is an automatic bodily function that is controlled by the respiratory center of the brain. Breathing in makes your blood cells to receive oxygen and release carbon dioxide. Improper breathing can result in upset the exchange of oxygen and carbon dioxide and this can make one anxious, feel fatigued, have panic attacks and even experience other physical and emotional disturbances.

The importance of relaxation response

When you relax, you breathe through your nose in a slow, even and gentle manner. A relaxed breathing pattern can calm the nervous system controlling the involuntary functions of the body.

The following are the changes that can be caused by controlled breathing;

- Controlled breathing will help you lower your blood pressure and heart rate.
- The level of stress hormones in the blood will be reduced.
- Lactic acid building up in muscle tissue will be reduced.
- You will experience increased energy in the body.
- Your oxygen and carbon dioxide levels in the blood will be balanced.
- Your immune system will be improved.
- You will generally feel calm and wellbeing.

How Can Breathing Contribute to Stress, Anxiety, And Panic?

Most are usually not conscious of the way we are breathing. As we all understand, the primary role of breathing is to promote the absorption of oxygen and the expulsion of carbon dioxide. Generally, we have two types of breathing patterns, thoracic / chest breathing and diaphragmatic / abdominal breathing. When we are anxious, one thing about our breathing is that we tend to take rapid, shallow breaths which usually come directly from the chest. This is referred to as the chest or thoracic breathing. Diaphragmatic breathing is breathing that comes from the diaphragm. This is a more effective and efficient way of breathing. This breathing can lead to feelings of relaxation. Many times, when we are anxious, we tend to breathe in this manner, but I know you have never been keen to even realize that. Well, when you breathe with your chest, the oxygen and carbon dioxide levels in the body are upset and as a result, you will have an increased heart rate, muscle tension, dizziness, and other physical sensations. When your blood is not properly oxygenated, a stress response signal may be generated, and this may contribute to panic attacks and anxiety.

Diaphragmatic Breathing

This breathing is a great way of reducing stress. You can follow the following instructions to get started;

- Find a nice comfortable place and sit in a comfortable position. Now close your eyes and in the process, collect all your attention to focus on your body and breath.

- Using your nose, inhale deeply to allow your abdomen to fill with air making your abdomen to be gently expanding out. Now, exhale this air by releasing it all through your nose in a relaxed and slow manner.

- Right below the navel on your abdomen, place one hand and then place the other hand on the upper part of your chest. Inhale deeply through your nose and exhale through your nose. While doing this, try to feel the coldness of the air you are inhaling and the warmth of the air you are exhaling.

- Now, while breathing in and out through your nose, I also want you to give your focus on shifting your breath so that you be able to feel the rising and the falling of your breathing in your abdomen. Ensure that your abdomen rises and falls more than your chest. While taking a deep breath, in through your nose, send some of this air through the back of your throat and down your belly. As you exhale through your nose, let your abdomen to slowly deflate.

- With your conscious focus on the rising and falling of your abdomen, take three more slow deep breaths. Now, continue with this breathing pattern fully and deeply. As you breathe allow and trust your body as the breath slows down and becomes more relaxed.

Deep breathing has benefits extending beyond in-the-moment stress relief. Researchers suggest that deep, yogic breathing serves an important role in balancing the autonomic nervous system which is responsible for the regulation of involuntary body functions like control of the body temperature and bladder functions. This is important because it may ease symptoms of stress-related disorders. Furthermore, it may also ease symptoms of health conditions like anxiety, depression, general stress, and post-traumatic stress disorder.

Getting Breath Focus

While breathing deeply, pictures some images in your mind or repeat phrases and words to help you feel more relaxed. I prefer, you can focus on your favorite color while going about your favorite relaxation exercise. Purple or deep blue is one of the most common color.

- If your eyes are open, close them.
- Take a few big deep breaths.
- While breathing in, you can imagine the process of air filling your lungs and being absorbed in the blood cells. Also, imagine that the air you are breathing in has a sense

of calm and peace. While breathing, try to feel this air throughout your body.

- Again, while breathing out, try to imagine that the air is leaving with all your tension and stress.

- Now, while breathing in, you can use the word or phrase you chose. You can also just picture the color you chose in your mind. For instance, as you breathe in, you can say in your mind, " I want a peaceful and calm life." and while breathing out, you can say, "I breathe out my stress and tension".

- Do this for ten to twenty minutes.

Equal Time for Breathing In And Breathing Out

This is an exercise that will help you match and balance the length of your breathing in and breathing out. With time as you practice deep breathing, you will be able to increase how long you breathe in and out at a given time.

- Sit in a comfortable position either in a chair or on the floor.

- As you breathe in through your nose, count some five seconds.

- Again, as you breathe out, count some five seconds.

- Repeat this several times.

After doing this for some time, you will feel comfortable with the five-second counts. You can then proceed to increase the length of your breath. You can try breathing in and outlasting for 10 seconds each.

Progressive Muscle Relaxation

This is a breathing technique where you breathe in while tensing a muscle group and then breathe out while releasing this muscle group out. This is a special technique that helps one to relax physically as well as mentally.

- Lie down comfortably on the floor.
- Breathe deeply to relax.
- Now, as you breathe in, tense your feet muscles.
- As you breathe out, release the tension in your feet.
- Secondly, you can breathe in while tensing your calf muscles.
- Now, you can again breathe out while releasing the tension in your calves.
- Repeat this while working your way up to your entire body. You can do this by tensing each muscle group. This includes starting with your legs, move to your belly, the chest then to your shoulders, arms, fingers and then neck and face.

Modified Lion's Breath

This is a breathing exercise that wants you to imagine that you are a lion. In this exercise, you will let all of your breath out through your mouth. What you need to do is just to open your mouth big.

- Get into a comfortable position in a chair or on the floor. Sit comfortably.

- Breathe in through your nose such that your belly is all filled up with air.

- Do this until you can't breathe in anymore. Now, open your mouth fully and then breathe out all the inhaled air with an "Ahh" sound.

- Repeat this several times over.

Relaxation Technique # 2: Body Scan Meditation

Body scan meditation is a meditation where you focus your attention on your various body parts. It is similar to muscle body relaxation because you will have to start down your feet as you work moving upwards. However, the difference is that instead of repetitive tensing and relaxing different muscle groups, you just give your focus and attention on the way each of your parts feels and you do this without labeling the sensations from this experience as bad or good.

It involves the following steps:

- While lying on your back, ensure that your legs are uncrossed and your arms are in a relaxed position at your side. Close your eyes. Now, give your focus and attention on breathing for about 2 to 3 minutes or above until you start to feel relaxed.

- Turn all your attention on your toes (you can start with your right foot). Be keen to note if there is any sensation on your toes while continuing to give your focus and attention on your breathing. Try to imagine that each of the deep breath you breathe in is flowing to your toes. Take five or more seconds to focus on this area.

- After this, now move your focus and attention to the soles of your feet (we are still on your right foot). Carefully and keenly note the sensations you are feeling in this body part. Imagine that each of the air you breathe in is flowing from the sole of your feet foot. Do this for some 1 to 2 minutes and then shift your focus to the ankle and then repeat the same. Now that you have mastered how the whole process is done, proceed to your calf, then your knee, move up to your thighs and the hip while repeating the same procedure. Do the same to your left leg. Once done with your legs, proceed up to the torso, moving through your abdomen and lower back, then to your chest and upper back and then to your shoulders. Again, you should be keen to identify any area in your body that seems to the pain you or to make you feel uncomfortable or painful.

- Now that you have done all these and completed body scan, take some few minutes and relax while in stillness and silence. Note how your entire body feels. Are you feeling relaxed and more released of your worries? Well done! Everything is now ok! You can open your eyes you slowly and stretch your body.

Relaxation Technique #3: Visualization

Visualization also referred to as guided imagery is a traditional meditation where an individual is made to image a scene that makes them feel more at peace and free and ready to let go of all their anxiety and tension. Depending on your preferences, choose the setting that you feel is the most calming to you. You can choose some nice silent tropical beach, a hilltop with nice scenery or your favorite childhood spot. If you don't know how to practice visualization on your own, you can choose a smartphone application or downloaded audio instructions. Any of these two will guide you through the process (imagery process). Visualization can also be done in silence or through listening aids like some soothing music, but all of this depends on your preferences. I usually prefer the sound made by ocean waves or birds and air on a hill.

Practicing Visualization

I would like you to close your eyes gently and then imagine the picture and feel of your most restful and peaceful place. Now, as vividly as you can, picture everything you can see, everything you can hear, feel, taste and smell. Look at these things in your mind and take it beyond the way you would look at a photograph. Note that visualization works best when as many sensory details as possible are incorporated. Let us consider this example;

Suppose you are on a quiet lake and you are about to dock, you can visualize the following;

- See water ripples moving away slowly.

- See some beautiful golden sun setting on the far end over the wáter.

- Smelling some fresh flowing air with the smell of pine trees.

- Taste the pure, fresh air.

- Feel some cold freshwater with sand beneath your bare feet.

- Hear the singing of birds.

Relaxation Technique #4: Self-Massage

I know you are already aware of the benefits that come with a professional massage regarding stress reduction, pain-relieving or even easing of muscle tension. However, what I am sure of is that you are not aware that you are able to experience similar benefits while at home or your places of work by simply practicing self-massage or doing massage with someone you love. You can dedicate some few minutes just to massage yourself on your couch or at your desk. I prefer that you do it on your couch or bed after having a stressful day at work. I think that you can use a scented lotion or aromatic oil for self-massage. Now that you have learned deep breathing techniques and mindfulness, you can choose to combine either deep breathing or mindfulness with self-massage.

Let's have a look at a 5-minute simple self-massage that will help to relieve you from stress.

Often, by combining different strokes, one is able to perfectly relieve muscle tension. Therefore, using the edge of the lower side of your hands, try gentle chops or tapings with your fingers. You can also use cupped palms. Using your fingertips, exert pressure on muscle knots. Squeeze or pound across your body muscles. You can also try moving smoothly in a long but light manner with your fingertips across your muscles.

In this short session, let's give our focus on the neck and the head self-massage:

- Begin by kneading your neck and then the back muscles of your shoulders. Make a fist that is not firm and then press swiftly moving upwards and downwards on your neck (both back and sides). Then next, using your thumbs, slowly massage the tiny circles found at your skull's base. Using your fingertips, continue with the massage to the rest of your scalp. After this, now tap your fingers against your scalp and do this as you move from front then to the back and then over sides as well.

- After finishing this, now move to massage your face. To do this, make several tiny circles using your thumb or fingertips paying a lot of attention to the jaw muscles, forehead and temples. Using your two middle fingers, slowly massage moving up to the bridge of your nose as you move up over your eyebrows than to your temples.

- In the final step, close your eyes and loosely cup one hand or both over your face and slowly breathe in and out for some ten to 30 seconds.

Relaxation Technique #5: Mindfulness Meditation

In recent years, this form of meditation has become very popular. It has gained popularity and endorsements from some of the most known psychologists, celebrities and even leading businesspeople. Mindfulness meditation is a meditation practice that teaches you that you should stop worrying about your future or dwell on your past and instead switch your mind and attention to focus on a single repetitive action like your breathing. Mindfulness meditation also encourages that you follow your internal thoughts and sessions and then release all of them.

Steps for Mindfulness Meditation

- Find a silent place that you feel assured that you will not be distracted or interrupted.

- Find a comfortable chair and sit comfortably with your back straight.

- Close your eyes and then find something repetitive to focus on. You can choose to focus on how you breathe. Feel the sensation coming from the air flowing in through your nostrils and feel the movement of your diaphragm. Also, feel the sensation of the warm air leave ours through your nose or mouth and the rising and falling of your belly. Repeat this throughout the meditation process.

- As you meditate, pay less attention to the distracting thoughts that may be going through your mind. You should also pay less attention to how well you are doing. In any case, thoughts are trying to interfere with your relaxation session, keep your mind calm, don't struggle to fight them, instead, gently shift your attention and take them back to the point where you focused on. Don't make any judgment.

Chapter 7
Improving Self-Confidence

Godfrey is a high school dropout who, due to financial problems, did not manage to proceed with his college education. Godfrey finished his high school education in 2013. Since his childhood, he has always had a passion to become a journalist. He relocated from his rural home and moved to Washington DC after losing his parents in 2014. Upon arriving in Washington, he knew he had to do anything to survive and make it in life. Back in high school, he was one of the best actors in school drama competitions. He had interests in joining the Washington cinema group which dealt with the acting of high school set books. Godfrey knew that joining this group was not going to be easy, but he had to give a try. Two weeks before the first audition, the participating candidates were already selected and instructed to each was told rehearse on specific characters in the book *An Enemy of the People by Henrik Ibsen*. Godfrey was instructed to play the role of *Peter Stockmann*. He knew that this was an opportunity for him. He had to give it his best despite having specialized to act novels and with a poor English accent. He believed in himself and when auditions came, he was one of the best candidates and was absorbed for this position.

After working with the Washington Cinema Group for two years moving up and down acting in all sorts of schools in Washington DC, he now wanted to pursue what he loved most: journalism. Luckily enough, there was a job vacancy in one of the top local radio stations. On the interview day, he dressed smartly and went for it. There were very many candidates, almost 20. Godfrey recalls that most of these candidates had a high education profile and had worked with some major radio stations. The interviewers began by asking those candidates with a degree in Media and Communication to step aside. Those who did not have were thanked for coming and told to try next time. Interestingly, Godfrey despite not having a degree in Media and Communication, stepped aside with those who had. In the next step, the interviewers again requested that those with a degree in Media and Communication and have worked with any radio station to step aside. Those who have not worked with any media station were thanked and told to try next time. Godfrey again moved to the side and stood with the group that had a degree and had worked in a radio station. Godfrey had confidence and believed in himself. Godfrey says "This is what I have always wanted despite having no experience or not the relevant papers. After all, it's just an interview, what will they do to me if they realize that I don't have all these requirements? They won't beat me. I will just be told to leave. I must give it a try."

Now when the time came for the candidates to hand in their resumes and certificates showing their qualifications, Godfrey stood confidently and told the interviewing team "I have none of the documents or requirements you have been looking for, but I believe I am the right candidate for this job position. I believe that I have all the qualities you have been looking for." The Interviewers were amazed and that is how Godfrey got his journalism job. He was on probation for 6 months and later on absorbed.

What Is Self Confidence and Why Is It important?

Self-confidence refers to the feeling of trusting your abilities, judgments, and qualities. Self-confidence plays a very important role in your health and psychological well-being. By having a healthy level of self-confidence, you can become successful in your personal, social and professional life.

More often, there are times that we fail to achieve our objectives. Well, such times can make us easily believe that we are not good enough or even feel that we do not have the ability. However, one fact is that the difference between success and failure should never be attributed to any lasting ability. Success and failure can be attributed to the lack of necessary skills at that particular time or at that very moment. But the moment you learn that skill, you are good to achieve anything. The biggest factor that will determine your success heavily relies on your self-confidence. Relating to a popular phrase by Sir Henry Ford; "Whether you choose to believe that you can do it, or you choose to believe that you cannot do it; you are right." Self-confidence is an important pillar that will help you to achieve your objectives and goals in life. As the level of your self-confidence grows, you will also have growth in the size of your goals and ambitions. No person is born with limitless self-confidence. I know you have been able to see some people with exception confidence levels and even admired them. The fact is that these people you see around who have incredible self-confidence were not born like that. It is simply because they have worked over the years to build it. Self-confidence is an essential part of humanity.

One thing that you will note about people who believe in themselves is that they are not always afraid to try out new things. People like Albert Einstein, Isaac Newton, Michael Faraday, and Nikola Tesla are people who believed in themselves. They believed in their capabilities and judgments and that is why they were able to try out new things. Now, copying these people, whether you are applying for a new job or job promotion or enrolling for a gym class, the key thing is believing in yourself and putting yourself. When you have self-confidence, you can like yourself and even be willing to take greater risks to achieve your goals. You are also able to think positively about the future. When you have low self-confidence or when you lack self-confidence, you are likely to have thoughts and feelings that you are unable to achieve your goals and dreams. You are also likely to have negative perspectives about yourself.

How Can You Build Self Confidence?

- **Cultivating a Good Attitude**

    The first step towards building self-confidence is by identifying your negative thoughts and then turning them to positive thoughts. The negative thoughts in us may sound like " I will fail", "I cannot do this", "no one is interested to hear what I am saying." Take your time to assess your inner voice particularly those pessimistic and unhelpful voices that hold you back and stops you from achieving greater self-confidence levels and high self-esteem. Turn all these voices and thoughts to positive thoughts and voices. You can turn these voices by saying things like "If I work on it, I can be successful", "I am going to give it a try", "People will listen to me" etc.

- **Maintain a positive support network**

It is good that you connect with people who are close to you to help you have an uplifting perspective. Stay away from people who make you feel bad. Some of your close friends or even a family member can make you feel bad especially if they constantly make negative remarks on you or negatively criticizes you. These are opinions that can be destructive and may impact negatively on your self-confidence. Therefore, take some time to think about the people who make you feel great. Think about people who give you the room to express yourself, your thoughts and feelings free when with them. These are the people you need to associate with. Make a goal to spend more time with them because they will support and uplift your self-confidence.

- **Eliminate reminders of your negativity**

It is also good that you try as much as you can to avoid spending much of your time around things or people that can provoke bad feelings in you. These things can be reminders from your past life experiences that made people look at you in a particular way or some clothing that no longer fits you because you are fat or thin or even some places that never made you realize your goals. Although it may be hard to eliminate these thoughts, you can, however, focus on how you can cut your losses.

- **Identify your talents**

Each and every person has something that they are good at. Take your time to discover what you are good at and you feel you can excel in. Focus on this talent. Permit yourself to be proud of your talent. Express yourself with this talent. If you are a footballer, give it your best and take pride while playing. You can also find the other things that you enjoy doing and cultivate talent in them. When you add a variety of hobbies and interests, you not only improve your self-confidence, but you also increase your chances of meeting people who you are compatible with. Secondly, following your passion will make you feel unique and accomplished and this can build your self-confidence.

- **Accept Your Imperfections**

Trying to be perfect will only inflict pain on you. It is not a must you be perfect. No one has ever been perfect, and no one will. Instead of focusing on being perfect, focus to try you best. From there, you can focus to learn from your experiences and strive to become better. It is good to understand that once you can do something, you always have the chance to improve it. As you get feedback from other people or some results or the world at large, you get to review them and identify areas of you need to improve on. Whether it is a skill, a product or a personal trait, feedbacks will help you to improve the loopholes. If you wait to be perfect yet you are not taking any action, then you will never start.

- **Stop Comparing Yourself with Others**

Comparisons are never healthy. There are many ways that at times we just end up comparing ourselves to others. We tend to compare how we look, what we earn, where we live, how we dress etc. Comparing yourself to others will only make you jealous and distract your self-esteem. Particular, you should, by all means, avoid paying attention to compare your skills, wealth, achievements, possessions and attributes to others. This may make you think that other people have more or are better than you and in the end; your confidence will be eroded. Anytime you find yourself trying to compare with others, cut off such thoughts and remind yourself that it is not a healthy practice.

Remember that everyone is running their race.

- **Dress Smart**

Many times, when you dress inappropriately, you just feel like everyone is looking at you in some suggestive manner that may end up affecting your self-esteem. If you lack confidence, the easiest and best way to boost it is by simply dressing with authority. Dressing smartly will make the people you interact with to perceive you like somebody important and you will start feeling like one. In normal situations, smart outfits are associated with an international symbol of status regardless of the country you are in or you are coming from. I prefer that you choose decent nice suits, nice shoes, shirts and other accessories like a watch. They will help in boosting your self-confidence.

- **Be comfortable with fear**

I know you may think or imagine that people with a high level of self-confidence are never fearful. This assumption is not true. It is good that you start looking at your growing edge. For instance, your fear may be speaking in front of many people, introducing yourself to someone or even asking for a pay rise from your boss. Once you become able to confront your fears, you will by default gain self-confidence.

Chapter 8
Don't Be Strict with Yourself

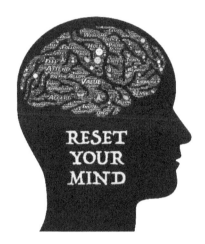

Why are you so hard on yourself? Stop being overly critical of yourself; you ought to know it is closely connected to low self-esteem issues. Although being self-critical is a trait associated with successful achievers, it is a double-edged sword. Even though the road of highly critical individuals is lined with success, it doesn't miss the stress that accompanies self-criticism. They will often suffer from issues such as insecurities and self-doubt. We understand that we all have trouble with being proud and content of ourselves. And it doesn't help in the long run if we are continually telling ourselves that we are not meeting our set expectations. We need to learn how to be better with ourselves, to learn how to motivate ourselves without pushing too hard.

We understand the objective of being critical of oneself is to be better and stay motivated to continue being energized to pursue our goals. However, to get here, we need to understand what behaviors we have that make us too critical ourselves. We will review that help you evaluate if you are critical of yourself.

They include:

- **You beat yourself up for mistakes that have minimal consequences**

We have all made mistakes, and most of the time, these mistakes are so small that they have minimal consequences. For example, you always have to check on the expiration date of products before you purchase them, but on this one occasion, you forgot to check. After you get home, you realize that the product will expire in three days. Then you start berating yourself on not observing the rules you keep for yourself. Although it's a minor mistake you spend time thinking over a small mistake that will have no major consequence in your life.

- **Even after you correct the mistake, you still criticize yourself**

We have all sent an email with a mistake or with no necessary attachments. Although you will apologize to the recipient after you notice it, you will start criticizing yourself because of not catching the mistake earlier. Even though this is not the first email you have sent with a mistake, why criticize yourself? You have already rectified the mistake, why don't you give yourself a break?

- **You rarely take self-care seriously**

Have you ever kept bumping your self-care priorities down your to-do list for other things? If you have, it seems you are having trouble taking care of yourself. Imagine you have a mattress that you find to be uncomfortable, but because your schedule is busy you keep bumping off your plan to buy a new one from your to-do list. You know that this decision will hurt your back and make your life miserable, but you decide to do it because you are busy. Giving yourself sleepless nights is not going to make you more effective. However, it will make you more irritable and susceptible to stress.

- **You find fault in yourself even when it is someone's fault**

Do you see fault in yourself when something has gone wrong even though it's someone else's fault? For example, when your teammate fails to follow through, do you blame yourself for not reminding them? Furthermore, if you are too critical of yourself, you will not confront when things when they go wrong. Instead, you will chicken out or second guess your decision to speak up.

- **You focus on unaccomplished goals**

So, you have a doctorate, a beautiful family and a well-paid job that you enjoy. However, you still focus on unaccomplished goals like not buying a home instead of being proud of what you have actually accomplished. It is important to have continuous goals but take some time to recognize what you have accomplished so far. We understand you have a lot more to accomplish but think about it will you be able to do so with stress and miserable life.

- **You speak in a negative tone**

Have you found yourself speaking in a more negative light than positive terms? For example, you attend a conference that required you to perform activities that are beyond your comfort zone. However, instead of recognizing the opportunity you had to explore your fears, you find yourself describing the experience as a bad one. Whether you realize it or not, speaking in negative terms makes you feel ashamed of yourself. Whenever you are speaking learn to pay close attention. Let us spread positivity.

- **You compare yourself to others**

Even when we have accomplished enough to feel the trophy cabinets, we still can't get enough. We still have to look up to that guy who has it all. It is important to strive and aim high from time to time. Although it becomes toxic when you start measuring your success against another individual. We all have different factors that will shape up our success. Sometimes, the more you focus on the other person's success against your own, the more you feel inadequate. Having issues with your self-esteem could lead to problems with anxiety and stress.

- **You are too independent**

In western culture, people who are independent or self-made are awarded and glorified. Although it is not a bad thing to be independent, the mindset will not allow you to ask for help. I know you are wondering how they are linked. Self-critical individuals will think that asking for help is a show of weakness or deficiency. Therefore, you will berate yourself when you have to ask for help making yourself shamed from exposing your deficiency. You have to understand even great inventors of our time seek help when something is not going well. Seeking help is not shameful, it is all in your mind.

- **You can't take compliments**

Someone compliments you on your new sweater, and without a pause, you tell them a negative comment to dispel their compliment. It comes off as cringeworthy when you do it too often. The compliment contradicts what we have been negatively telling ourselves to get off wearing the sweater. However, when you continue shooting down the compliments you give an impression that you do not appreciate how other people treat you or yourself. Your mind registers only the negativity you berate yourself. Therefore, leaving you anxious and stressed.

We understand that we can sometimes be our own worst enemy by being so much harder on ourselves than others. However, how does this affect you? Especially when your business or career is taking off. Failure in life is inevitable, and if you cannot stop being too critical of yourself, problems will arise. Once you have discovered that you are too critical of yourself you need to kill the negative thoughts you tell yourself. How are you going to do this?

- **Mind your thoughts**

You are so used to hearing your thoughts, and you can be oblivious to the message you send to your subconscious. Do you have negative thoughts? When you pay close attention to your thoughts, you may discover that you berate yourself when things are not working. Imagine with an estimate of 60,000 thoughts in a day, do you build yourself up or tear yourself down? If you find you are tearing yourself down, change that. Be the master of your thoughts and avoid sending negative subliminal information to your conscience. Learning to keep track of your thought patterns is one step to mastering how thinking affects your life.

- **Don't ruminate on your mistakes**

When you engage in problem solving, do not spend too much time thinking about it. This can be a self-destructive task. If you can't stop thinking about a problem, you will pull yourself down. However, there is a neat trick to train your mind to stop overthinking the problem. Get yourself involved in an activity that will temporarily distract you. Shut the negative thoughts from your mind and deny them the chance to negatively influence your thoughts.

- **Learn to advise yourself as you would to your friend**

Have you noticed how harder we are on ourselves than on others? You may end up berating yourself or you may call yourself an idiot for making a mistake. However, when you are talking to your friend or family it is unlikely you will do the same. When you are struggling with something, offer yourself some advice as you would to a friend. It will sound nicer and motivate you to continue trying to solve the problem. Furthermore, it will encourage your mind to take five you a break when you mess up.

- **Give yourself room for improvement**

Learning to accept your flaws and commit yourself to do better in the future will reduce being too critical on yourself. You will notice the big difference between thinking that you are not good enough and thinking there is room for improvement. For example, you might be up for a presentation at work, and you feel that your public speaking skills are not good. So, make a decision to improve them in the future. Accepting yourself with all the flaws while investing in the future you will make you better in the long run. It is easier to give yourself room for improvement than letting your mind tell itself that you are inadequate.

- **Avoid comparing yourself to others**

In this world, we have been taught to compete for everything. Whether it is the top spot in class or becoming the employee of the month, we are always competing. Before you compare yourself to others count your blessings. If you focus on your strengths, you will find out that you have a lot to offer and to be happy about. Also, you could develop awareness when you start comparing yourself. If you discover you are comparing yourself, tell your mind to stop it and start thinking of the goals you have achieved in the past and how happy you ought to be about them. By practicing regularly, you will start to be happier and less critical of yourself.

- **Learn how to accept compliments**

When we do not accept a compliment, we devalue ourselves as well as showing disrespect to the person kind enough to give us a compliment. First, we should learn to accept ourselves; start by writing down 10 traits you like about yourself. This will give you enthusiasm so that when someone gives you a compliment, you can add it to that list. Moreover, accepting is as easy as saying "thank you." In the future, you will find that accepting compliments not only encourages emotional growth but also helps defeat the negative thoughts your mind projects to your subconscious. Also, train yourself in giving others compliments on things striking about them. It will encourage positivity and mindfulness, which are positive traits to encourage positive emotional growth.

- **Don't let guilt eat you up**

Guilt is the main emotion we feel when we are too critical of ourselves. Imagine you forgot to send an email to someone on time, guilt will haunt you even after you have corrected the mistake. The situation is out of your control, but still, you figure out how to put the blame in yourself. Train your mind to shield you from thoughts that will induce guilt. At least you have made amends for the mistake, nobody could have done better. Also, train your mind to let go of the guilt once you apologize for your mistakes.

You need to understand why avoiding too much self-criticism will benefit you. Also, understand there are strategies you can pursue to help you stop being overly critical of yourself. Not only will these strategies make you feel better but also help you make informed decisions and waste less emotional energy. In turn, you will be more productive in the future. Also, being less critical of yourself requires you to prioritize your self-care, your mind and soul are as important as the physical body. Ensure you keep your thought in check by practicing mindfulness and taking a break when you get overwhelmed. Understand that you are your first friend, and if you make a mistake you need to treat yourself as you would treat your friend. Being less critical will improve your thoughts and encourage room for growth in the future.

Chapter 9
Learning about Your Body

Musculoskeletal System

When an individual is in an anxious state, muscles tend to become tense. The tension being experienced by the body is often a reflex reaction to anxiety. In most cases, it is always a way the body guards itself from injury or pain it predicts to incur.

The muscles of an individual tend to tense up at once in moments anxiety strikes him or her. The tension experienced in the muscles relaxes in the event the anxiety trigger passes. There certain moments that an individual's muscles are prone to be in a constant state of being on guard. The description of fits situation where one is having chronic anxiety attacks. There are several reactions that can be triggered in the event that the muscles are in constant periods of anxiety. These reactions have the potential of making an individual experience different kinds of anxiety disorders.

The body releases several signs when it is in a constant state of anxiety and the muscles are overly tense. The common reaction sign is always an individual having tense muscles in the head, neck, and shoulders. The second depiction of this state is migraine headaches. There are other musculoskeletal pains that are accompanied in events an individual experiences anxiety. They are pains that are experienced in the low and upper extremities of the body. They are prone to people who have employments.

There are millions of people across the world who suffer from quite painful secondary musculoskeletal disorders to other chronic conditions. There are other cases that the pain may have been triggered by injuries an individual may have had during their lifetime. There are several injuries that may make an individual be in a constant state of anxiety. There are moments that the healing of certain injuries can be accelerated by the thoughts of an individual. Having tense tissues in most cases has the potential of making an individual have a low rate of healing. The situation can pan out to be very dangerous for an individual if it is persistent for a long period of time. It can lead an individual to experience certain musculoskeletal chronic disorders.

There are several related techniques that have been discovered over the years. These relaxation methods can be very beneficial to an individual in so as to relieve anxiety from an individual. The most common ways that people use to relax these muscles include the usage of therapies. These therapies include both massage and mental therapies since they have shown great amounts of success. A person with a relaxed musculoskeletal system has a high potential of being happy and having good moods which are very important when an individual is handling his day to day activities.

Respiratory System

There is a major role that the respiratory is commonly known to perform at its best. The system is responsible for supplying oxygen to the cells of an individual and the removal of carbon dioxide from one's body. The air individual breaths incomes through the nose and passes through a person's larynx that is located at the throat. The air goes down the individual's trachea and gets into the lungs via the bronchi.

Anxiety and other strong emotions that an individual can encounter have high chances of being present in the respiratory system. There are common occurrences that have struck several people across the globe. They include individuals experiencing shortness in his or her breathing which is followed by a rapid form of breathing. During these moments, the airway between the lungs and nose tends to constrict. This is not a major problem for people who do not have major respiratory conditions. This is because the body has the potential of managing to extra work for an individual to breathe comfortably.

On the other hand, anxiety can be a horrible case for people who have respiratory diseases. The reason is that it has the potential of exacerbating breathing problems to an individual. The most common respiratory chronic conditions are asthma and chronic bronchitis. There are several types of research that have been conducted on the phenomenon. It was found that anxious situations such as the death of a loved one have the potential of making a person experience asthma attacks. There are several cognitive-behavioral strategies that have been set aside to help individuals in such moments.

Cardiovascular

The cardiovascular system of an individual is comprised of two major elements. These two major components are the heart and the blood vessels. Both of these components work hand in hand so as to provide an individual with oxygen and nourishment to his or her body organs. The intriguing part an individual has to know is that the two major cardiovascular have a way they coordinate in the event a person is in an anxious state so as to respond to the trigger.

There are several forms of anxiety triggers that can be described as short term and cute. These triggers include the likes of an individual failing to meet the meeting deadlines, being stuck in a jam or sudden braking to avoid an accident. These forms of anxiety trigger have the potential of an individual heart rate.

This is a result of the strong contractions of the muscles present in his or her heart. The situation is also caused by the release of the fight or fling hormones such as adrenaline and cortisol since they are messengers for this kind of situation.

There are vessels in an individual's body that are tasked with the role of directing blood to the large muscles of the body and one's hearts dilate. They are prone to increasing the amount of blood being supplied in these areas of the body. In return, this action often leads to an increase in blood pressure to a person's body. It is a characteristic of the flight or fight response of an individual's body. The situation clears in the event the anxiety trigger disappears and the body then cools down to its normal state.

Chronic anxiety can be defined as long-term and persistent occurrence of panic attacks. This condition has a detrimental effect on an individual's body. It has the potential of affecting the heart and blood vessels for a long period of time. The happenings of the increased flow of blood and palpitation of the heart have the ability to take a toll on an individual's body. In the long term, a person can end up suffering from stroke, hypertension or heart attacks because of the constant effect of anxiety on the cardiovascular system.

Anxiety attacks that are repeated and acute have the ability to influence the inflammation of the circulatory system. The problem tends to be worse when it comes down to the coronary artery. It is very important since it ties anxiety to heart attacks. There are several studies that have been done that signify that an individual's cholesterol levels can be determined by how he or she handles anxiety.

The risks that are presented with respect to heart attacks tend to vary among people. In general, heart attacks are more predominant in men than in women, though the fact is that anyone who is overly stressed is at increased risk of having a cardiac incident. As such, it is essential to take better care of heart health by promoting calming and soothing practices which can help regular pulsation, breathing and even blood pressure. Through this type of self-care, you can greatly reduce the likelihood of suffering from such an illness. Furthermore, taking care of your heart health can help you achieve better oxygenation thereby feeding your brain with oxygen-rich blood on a consistent basis.

Endocrine

There are several ways human being perceives when situations are uncontrollable, threatening or challenging. However, there is a special way in which the brain is able to initiate a flow of events that involve the hypothalamic-pituitary-adrenal (HPA) axis. It is the primary driver of the anxiety response in the endocrine system. The normal occurrence of this effect entails the increase in the production of the steroid hormone. The hormone being referred to is known as the glucocorticoids which are inclusive of a stress hormone known as the cortisol.

The HPA Axis

There are several happenings that go on in an individual's body is at the anxiety state. The process kick starts from a collection of nuclei known as the hypothalamus which is responsible for connecting the brain and the endocrine system. The hypothalamus signals the pituitary gland of an individual to release a certain hormone. The hormone release is responsible for the signal intercepted by the adrenal gland are located above an individual's kidney to produce more cortisol hormone.

The cortisol hormone is responsible for the increase in the quantity of available energy in an individual's body. This is made possible because it is able to mobilize the fatty acids and glucose that is always present in a person's liver. The cortisol hormone has a varying production across the day in a human body. It is often high in production in moments an individual is starting the day with high levels of energy and it declines with time as the energy levels decrease. It is a cycle that is accustomed to a human day in day out life. During moments of anxiety, this hormone is released in high contents to help an individual deal with the current situation that is ahead of them.

Anxiety and Health

The glucocorticoids which are inclusive of the cortisol are very important in an individual's body. They play a vital role in regulating a person's immune system and reductions of inflammations. This can be very advantageous in moments an individual is faced with anxious situations that can result in him or her incurring injuries. However, in moments the anxiety attacks are persistent; it can impair the communication between the HPA axis and the immune system of an individual. Several physical and mental conditions can be triggered such as metabolic disorders, anxiety disorders or chronic fatigue.

Gastrointestinal

The gut of an individual is filled with millions of neurons. Their functions of these neurons can be done by them in a fairly independent manner. They are also in constant communication with the brain of an individual. The constant communication with people is the best explanation for an individual who is constantly experiencing butterflies in or her stomach.

Anxiety has the potential of triggering several discomforts such as pain and gloating in the gut. These discomforts brought about by anxiety are easily experienced by several people across the globe. It is very important for an individual to know that the gut is inhabited with millions of bacteria. These bacteria have the potential of affecting an individual's thinking ability and his or her emotions. There are several instances that anxiety is associated with the change in the bacteria in the gut thus affecting someone's mood. Therefore, the nerves found in the gut have a strong influence on a person's brain and vice versa.

Experiencing anxiety in the early parts of life has a very detrimental impact on an individual. It has the influencing of changing an individual's development of his or her nervous system. This situation creates a worse situation which is altering an individual's body reaction to anxiety. The problem is very tricky since has the potentials leading an individual to experience.

Esophagus

There are two occurrences that can in the event an individual is stressed. He or she can eat high amounts of food or it can result in him or her to eat low amounts of food. There are other people who can end up using self-destructive substances such as alcohol or tobacco so as to help them get over the situation. The two substances are common in making an individual experiencing acid reflux or heartburn. The pain experienced in the gut is prone to increase each time an individual experiences anxiety attacks. There are other cases when swallowing food can be a difficult task when an individual is swallowing food in an event they are having anxiety attacks.

Stomach

The bloating, pain, and nausea caused by anxiety can be easily felt by an individual. A person may even go as far as vomiting in instances when anxiety attacks are severe. There are other cases that can be a sign of an individual is experiencing anxiety attacks. One individual can either have high levels or low levels of appetite. There are other forms of food that can make an individual enter an anxiety state in moments they are being digested or absorbed in an individual's body. There are several people who tend to believe anxiety has the potential of making a person experience ulcer attacks. The phenomena are true because of the increased level of acid production.

Bowel

Anxiety is characterized by pain and bloating that is experienced at the bowel of an individual. These are just a few justifications that are portrayed in the bowel by an individual who is experiencing anxiety. There are certain moments when an individual experiences diarrhea or constipation when faced with an anxiety attack. The reason behind this is because of the slow and disturbing movements of food in the body. There are moments that the pain induced by anxiety attacks can be painful since they are a result of muscle spasms.

Anxiety attacks are very troublesome because they affect an individual's intestines at the moment they absorb nutrients. The bloating might increase the absorption of gas in an individual's body. The other negative impact can be witnessed when it comes to the bacterial entrance to an individual system. It is possible when an individual is experiencing anxiety. It is because the situation has the potential of weakening the strong barrier that is present in the intestines. The barrier prevents bacteria from going into an individual's system.

There are some cases in which bacteria are taken in, but the immune system tends to tackle it. This is the major reason which answers why a person is not sick in most cases he or she experiences anxiety attacks. Constant occurrence of anxiety attacks can have a negative impact on an individual's health. They may lead to chronic bowel disorders such as irritable bowel syndrome.

Nervous System

The nervous system of an individual has several divisions. There is a central division that is encompassed with the brain and the spinal cord of a person. There is a peripheral division that contains the somatic and autonomic systems. This nervous system is related to having a direct role in the physical responses to anxiety. The autonomic system is further divided into two sympathetic and parasympathetic nervous systems (SNS and PNS). The SNS is responsible for the production of the flight or fight hormone in the event an individual is anxious.

The body shifts its energy towards the preparation to tackle the anxiety trigger. During these moments, the SNS is responsible for sending signals to the adrenal glands that release adrenaline and cortisol hormones. The two hormones are responsible for several happenings when they are combined with actions from the autonomic nerves. They are responsible for the increase in heart palpitation, increase in the respiratory rate, inadequate on other parts of the body and impaired digestive functions.

The response that is experienced by an individual is fairly sudden. The major reason behind this depiction of anxiety is because it prepares the body to handle the danger about to happen. It is a short-term effect in most cases. The body tends to move to its normal state after the anxiety trigger disappears. The state where an individual recover is triggered by the PNS. It is described as having a reverse effect on the SNS. They are very powerful parts of the brain because they an individual to regulate anxiety.

Chronic attacks of anxiety can be very detrimental to a person. The potential of an individual's body getting drained is quite high. The central nervous system also has a way in which it reacts when anxiety is present in an individual's body since they trigger stress responses as it regulates an individual's autonomic nervous system. It also plays a critical role in the interpretation of the impending danger.

Male Reproductive System

It is greatly influenced by the nervous system of an individual. The sympathetic nervous system part is tasked with arousal while the parasympathetic part is responsible for relaxation. The male reproductive system is often related to arousal in moments of anxiety. This is because the flight or fight hormones produced lead to the production of testosterone that makes the sympathetic nerves. Cortisol which a hormone that is released during anxiety, has the potential of affecting a man's functioning of the reproductive system.

Sexual Desire

The sexual drive of a man can be affected to deteriorate to low levels because of anxiety attacks. Persistent chronic attacks can lead to an individual experiencing erectile dysfunction.

Reproduction

Anxiety can make the production of sperms to be low causing problems while trying to conceive. There are several types of research that have been done to prove this phenomenon right. The study showed that men who had experienced two or more anxiety attacks that were severe, their sperms had a very low ability to swim. It was also found that the sperm size of this individual was small compared to men who had not suffered from anxiety attacks. The movement's anxiety attacks are persistent, man testis, urethra and prostate gland can be affected.

Female Reproductive System

Menstruation

There are certain moments the menstrual flow can be affected by being delayed when a lady is anxious. It is very common for adolescent girls.

Sexual Desire

Anxiety can be depicted in women in the event sexual desires diminish. It is because the body fully concentrates on the danger that is impending.

Pregnancy

Anxiety can have a very big influence on a woman's reproductive plan. This is a common phenomenon across the globe. There are have been several situations that impending danger has affected woman delivery dates. Anxiety states have made some women experience miscarriages or early deliveries.

Chapter 10
Achieving Self-Awareness

What is self-awareness?

To live beyond your fears, anxious feelings, worries, and negative thoughts is the ultimate goal for many folks. As such, self-awareness is one of the essential things that you need to cultivate in your life. But what does it mean to be self-aware? Having self-awareness means being fully aware of your personality. It means that you are excellent at realizing your weaknesses and strengths, your beliefs and thoughts, your motivations, and your emotions.

Being aware of yourself brings self-knowledge, and having self-knowledge makes you understand other people with ease, and also detect how they perceive you. Self-awareness creates a platform for you to make adjustments to some habits, beliefs, or behaviors that may be impacting negatively on your interpersonal relationships.

When you achieve self-awareness, your behaviors, habits, thought, and perceptions begin to change. Changed thoughts and interpretations lead to a change in your mentality. A changed mental state begins to alter your emotions, which enhances your emotional intelligence. All these changes are essential for your overall success in social settings and work-related scenarios. You will be able to monitor, identify, and rectify any negative emotions and thought which fuel your negativity and bad mood.

Self-awareness leads to changing habits

Self-awareness is an essential step if you want to build a life that you want, as you can pinpoint your emotions and passions, and understand how your personality can help you in living the life you want for yourself. You can make the necessary changes as early as possible when you recognize where your emotions and thoughts are leading you. You will give your life the right direction by understanding your behavior, feelings, ideas, and the way you perceive yourself in the light of the world. Self-awareness will enable you to have a happier outlook in life, as you can monitor and eliminate negative thoughts and emotions that fuel your negativity, anxiety, fear, worrisome thoughts, and unbalanced mood.

Self-awareness is critical in leadership education, social work, counseling, and almost any other area of our lives that entail interpersonal relations with colleagues, friends, spouse, and family. Don't just sit around and do nothing when you feel that there are some areas of your life that you need to explore and become more aware of as most people do. As a quick first step, you can look at a relative scale, so that you can know where you fit on it in comparison to other people. Then you can begin to work on yourself from there to eliminate harmful things that weigh you down in your life.

It is self-awareness that makes it possible for you to accept your weaknesses, faults, circumstances, situation, and events that surround your life. Such acceptance is crucial and marks a long journey of self-acceptance. The moment you have accepted yourself the way you are, you get the strength to focus on various techniques for self-improvement.

Understand your life story

For several years now, psychologists have been focusing on a new area of study known as narrative identity. The main premise behind the study is that the story you tell yourself about your life won't just shape your personality – it will be your personality. The story you tell yourself about your life is your narrative identity. Your future goals and achievements, together with your current passions and motivation, will be dictated by the understanding you have on your narrative.

What do you say about yourself? What is your self-drive? Research shows that your mental and physical health will improve if you look at your tough life experiences and write about them aiming to learn from your past. Your level of self-awareness will be defined by how you confront challenges that come your way on a daily basis.

So how do you identify your true north by looking at your personal story? You need to look at your life story right from childhood. Look at the people you interacted with, the events you hated or loved, and other experiences that impacted your life as you grew up. Identify the things which you were passionate about and the motivations which kept you going while growing up. Were you anxious, talkative, introverted, extroverted, or did you love attending social gatherings? Then look at what happened along the way and note the experiences which impacted your life to make you the kind of person you are today. That way, you will be able to know where the rain started beating you and take the necessary steps to change your narrative.

Take an objective look at yourself

It is a difficult process to try to see yourself as you really are, but it is advantageous if you make the right efforts towards realizing yourself. After being able to see yourself objectively, you can practice and learn to accept yourself and then begin the process of improving yourself going into the future. But how can you look at yourself objectively?

- The goal here is not to compare yourself to your friends or colleagues at work, but to know what really makes you tick. Try and write down on a piece of paper your perceptions in an attempt to identify your current understanding of yourself and the world around you. Begin by writing down things that you are excellent in, and then write or describe areas that you feel that you need to improve.

- Think of things that make you proud in life. Think of things which you have done so far, which have attracted outstanding compliments either in social settings or at the workplace.

- Reflect on your childhood. What used to make you happy in those days? Think about the things which have changed, and those that have remained the same. Then try to think of experiences and events which have bought about such changes.

- Let your friends and colleagues know that you want them to be honest with you. No flattery or battering words on how they feel about or perceive you. If they are legitimate, take what they tell you seriously and focus on making the necessary changes.

The net effect of this honest, objective look at self will be rewarding. You will emerge stronger, with a fresh new perception on your life, yourself, and the world around you.

Keep a journal of your thought and feelings

Documenting your thoughts, emotions, beliefs, and goals can be an excellent way to track yourself. Recording your thoughts on a journal relieves your mind of such thoughts and ideas, clearing it up to create space for fresh ideas and information. Practice this by setting some time aside every day to write about your emotions, thoughts, and feelings for the day. Also, make sure to record your successes and failures, and you will find yourself beginning to move forward and grow in what you can achieve.

As you write, picture yourself being a famous person, rising above your fears and anxiety. Let your brain get to work and transform you. See yourself as a leader, having mastered public speaking skills, and being confident enough to stand before significant social gatherings and give outstanding talks. As these ideas continue to come to mind, document them in your journal, and practice them daily. Write down the essential things which are affecting your life, and how you can incorporate the help of other people in your life to rise above your weaknesses.

Journal your shortcomings, and the positive steps you can take to become stronger in the areas that you are weak. Jot down your mantra, and personal or business statement that reminds you of who you are and whom you are trying to become. Write down the techniques and strategies which you intend to use to counter any negativity, stress, and worrisome thoughts that try to infiltrate your mind.

By learning to document the good and the bad that crosses your mind daily, you can gain insight on who you are, and learn to focus on the good, while keeping the bad at bay. You will become more self-aware and maximize your efforts pursuing to become the kind of person you want to be right now.

Write down your plans, priorities, and your goals

This will enable you to track your achievements. Putting down your ideas and turning them into a step by step, achievable goal is the right place to start. Looking at the big idea sometimes can be overwhelming. But when you break it down into smaller daily goals, you can achieve it by tackling it head-on with a plan. Setting priorities will also help you set boundaries and avoid getting lost in the middle of a busy schedule.

Remember that if you have got no plan for your life, you have already planned to fail. Sometimes, you might do a lot in life, but because you don't have a program that governs your measurable goals, you may end up feeling like you have failed on your responsibilities and duties. This can trigger unnecessary fears, worries, and anxiety. But if you have a plan, and you have set achievable daily goals, you have a way to measure your progress. You will avoid feeling as if you have done nothing when in real sense you have done enough for the day or thinking that you have done a lot, while in real sense you have done very little.

Setting goals will also help you to avoid overworking or underworking. You will be able to strike a balance between time for work, time for leisure, time for family, and time for focusing on self-improvement by reading insightful books and articles.

So, don't weigh yourself down by looking at the huge task and begin to think that it is beyond your capacity and potential. This makes you approach it with a defeatist attitude and awaken unnecessary anxiety or stress. Have a plan, break it down into mini-goals and give each goal priority so that you can achieve them in an orderly manner and avoid getting lost in the middle of everything.

Writing down your goals, plans, and priorities, and documenting how you intend to accomplish them is very crucial if you are to achieve self-awareness. This is especially when it comes to an understanding of your potentials and what you can do for yourself.

Perform daily self-reflection

You cannot achieve self-awareness without performing self-reflection. This demands that you set aside some time regularly, to give an honest look at yourself as a person or as a leader. This is easier said than done but committing yourself to this practice will help you improve immensely. It takes time to perform self-reflection, and it requires you to be in a quiet place with yourself to reflect and think.

The world if fast-paced, and there is a lot of information coming from all quarters. In this busy world of work, business, social media and family life, it is easy to succumb to the demands of a busy schedule and forget to remind yourself of who you are, and where you are going. That is how so many people get lost in the middle of everything and ignore the values and principle which make them tick.

Technology has advanced a lot, and there is an endless flow of data and information thought the various electronic gadgets that we own today. A lot is going on in your portable devices such as your mobile phone, laptop, and tablet. When you get home, you get bombarded with a myriad of information that flows from countless TV shows and channels, each competing to control your mind and influence you in one way or another.

That is why you need to perform daily reflection. It is a demanding activity, but richly rewarding. Being overwhelmed with information can make you forget who you really are and begin to live after the world's views and opinions or find yourself succumbing to the spews of the media in the air. Start by putting aside at least twenty minutes every day before going to bed and remind yourself of your values, priorities, beliefs, fears, plans, goals and any other principles that form the foundation of your life.

Self-reflection will help you sift the right from the wrong, the true from the false and the fact from the fiction. By reflecting on all the daily activities, you have engaged in, and the information you have come across throughout the entire day, you realize yourself more. Get an honest look at what drives your life so that you can avoid being altered by the world view to begin doing things that do not reflect who you are.

Practice meditation

This helps you to enhance your mindful awareness. Mostly meditation focuses on breath, but you can also do it by practicing regular lapses of reflection. As you meditate, stop and focus on your goal, successes, your failures, some obstacles that are hindering you from realizing your purpose, and the changes that you can make to improve yourself. You need a silent room or a quiet place in the woods. Focus on deep breathing and other relaxation techniques that bring peace to your life and clears your mind of any clutter on negativity, so that you can only focus on what is essential in your life.

However, meditation doesn't have to be formal all the time. You can find great moments of being mindfully aware of your life by engaging yourself in simple activities in the house that are less demanding. Some activities such as jogging, church activities, and washing dishes come with therapeutic serenity. During these simple activities, stop and meditate on your goals, what is working in your life, the obstacles hindering your success and what you are doing or can do to overcome them, and the different techniques and strategies that you can employ in your life to improve yourself and be more useful to your family, workplace and other areas of your social life.

Psychometric and personality tests

Taking such a test helps you to get a quick rough idea of what your traits are. These tests do not have the wrong or right answers. They only compel you to think of specific characteristics or qualities that closely describe you in relation to other people. Several tests are available for you to take for free online, such as the Myers-Briggs test or the Predictive Index.

Sometimes you need something to kick start your thinking. These tests are not meant to define you but give you a rough idea of your personality and character traits. They can act as a basis for you to start thinking about who you are as you will have something to peg your thoughts on. You can then begin working to achieve self-awareness from such a good foundation because you have an idea of your personality in relation to a sea of other individuals out there. Most of the time, you will find that you are not severely positioned, and you will be encouraged to work on areas that weight you down so that you can improve and achieve self-awareness from the light of the world.

Ask a friend you trust to describe you

The easiest way to know how other people think of you is to as a friend, a close family member, or a mentor to describe you shortly. Tell them to act as an honest mirror, and make them understand that you want a critical, open, and objective view. Let your friends give you an informal but honest perspective and allow them to feel free and safe as they do so.

Let your friends know that you want such an honest perspective to improve yourself, and tell them that by being honest, they are helping but not hurting you. Ask some questions about the view they have given you so that you can understand clearly. When you begin doing something that you want to change, ask your friends to bring it to your attention.

Ask for feedback from your colleagues at work

After getting some perspective form family and friends, get formal feedback from your colleagues at work. Precise feedback will allow you to reflect on your strengths and weaknesses. After going through the feedback process, put down on paper the surprise weaknesses or strengths that you did not recognize you had before. Promise yourself to work on areas in which your colleagues feel that you are weak, and don't get worked up when they point something which will not go down well with you. Remember that you need an honest opinion so that you can become more self-aware.

Adopt a lifestyle of regular exercise and physical activity

Physical activities come with a sense of therapeutic serenity to your mind, emotions, and physical body. It is a great way to unwind and clear any form of stress, cluttered negative thoughts, and feelings that lead to anxiety. A healthy body and a healthy mind are what you need to become more self-aware. With an excellent body shape, and an evident, strong mentality, you cannot mistake yourself. You will be able to think clearly and see yourself for who you are because you will have cleared negative thoughts and emotions which would have hindered you from thinking straight and appreciating your true self. Engaging in at least thirty minutes of physical activity every day is a great way to knock out any form of stress and depression in your life, which tends to hinder the journey towards achieving self-awareness. As you exercise, you also get an opportunity to reflect and meditate on your current and future life.

Final thoughts

As you can see, it can take quite some time before you get to the point of mastering your self-awareness and knowing yourself better. Depending on how you do it, it can take months or years as you try to reflect on your own, get the perspective of your friends, family members, and feedback from your colleagues at work. But building the necessary habits to aid you in becoming more self-aware will help you reap the long-term benefits.

It will have a positive impact on other aspects of your life, such as your interpersonal relationships, your social networks, and advancement in your career. Self-awareness will help you shun negativity, worrisome thought, unnecessary anxiety, stress and depression, which come as a result of being lost in the sea of other people's opinions and the views of the world concerning you.

Chapter 11
Surround Yourself with People Who Make You Feel Good

The people you associate with have a huge impact on how you feel about yourself and the things around you. The anxiety of the brain is particularly affected by people's opinions and their general actions around you. The success of keeping your mind free from negativity lies in knowing your purpose as someone who is struggling with anxiety. People you should be associating with are those that are doing better than you in anxiety management. These people could be your friends, relatives or peers. Sometimes people in your workplace can have an impact on your life outside work. It is quite difficult to avoid this kind of people, but you can find ways to go around those obstacles. For instance, you can decide to maintain a completely professional relationship with your colleagues at work, those that do not impact your life positively. The main goal is to give your mind the most conducive environment. You should stop at nothing until this purpose is achieved. If you cannot eliminate some people you consider toxic entirely from your circles, the best thing to do is to minimize your exposure to them. This means you will have to spend less time with them, and that little time spend with them should be closely monitored. Only pick positive things in the form of ideas and opinions from them.

There are numerous benefits of letting life happen for you instead of happening to you. The former means you are in control, everything is falling into place according to your expectations. If you have purposed to maintain a healthy mind, then the kind of expectations you should have include meeting people who will instill in you empowering beliefs and thoughts. You will then be able to make that happen by actually going out to meet them. The secret lies in developing effective techniques to pull those people into your circle without you appearing desperate and needy. Let it happen naturally, forcing things has never worked anywhere. If you do it right, they will actually end up thinking it was their own idea that you got close. Once they successfully fall into your trap, the hard part now becomes keeping them. Again, this is not that hard as you might think. We come back to our keyword-strategy. Get to know your new friends or associates then device appropriate ways to handle each of them. People are different so you will have to deal with each one of them differently. Some are difficult while others are simple, all that matters is for you to get the right people into your circles.

The first step in surrounding yourself with people that make you happy is by sorting the people in your circles. Start by identifying those that give you positive energy. People you feel safe, happy and motivated whenever you are around them and even after they have left. These kinds of people are the right ones for you, keep them. The second category is those that are negative and narrow-minded. You realize that immediately after meeting them, you feel fearful, irritated and drained. These are the kind of people you are going to cut off completely. Of course, doing this will be a challenge but it is something you must do for the sake of your mental health. You don't have to actually push them away in a rude manner, just reduce the amount of attention you give them, and this should happen in phases. If you have a friend you have kept for long, for example, and somehow you think they are a bad company, don't tell them outright that you are done with them. Reduce the number of times you hang out together to say, once a week, twice a month and eventually once or twice a year. The bond will automatically weaken over time until it is no more.

The following are tips that will help you surround yourself with the right people.

Increase your worth

Things that are worthless have a tendency to attract many people, the majority of them being mediocre ones. When you elevate your standards, you will be able to only attract the best kind of people. Brain anxiety results from many things among them idleness. Those people that always keep their minds preoccupied have a lower probability of experiencing anxiety. Keeping yourself busy with meaningful things and that is where you will meet like-minded people. Their level of maturity will be your benchmark. Learn how they solve their problems and try to apply the same. If you concentrate on petty things, on the other hand, you will only attract jokers and narrow-minded people. There is nothing new this person will teach you; they will probably pull you down to their level and laugh at you. They will give you a thousand reasons to give up on your relationship or that project you have been working very hard to finish.

As if that is not enough, they will show you their own methods of dealing with anxiety, and this might include engaging in alcohol and substance abuse. The best thing elevating your standards is that you will automatically repel everything else that is below you. You won't have to struggle to kick narrow-minded people out of your circles, they will get themselves out if they see they can't fit in anymore. Similarly, you won't struggle to bring in people with positive energy, they will be attracted by the light that comes from you. This is when you will pounce on them like a hungry lion and tap a little of their energy.

Get Someone That Already Has the Results

Dealing with the anxiety of the brain is a practical thing, not a theoretical one. Don't look for something where it doesn't exist. Before approaching someone about your problem, especially if the person is not a professional psychotherapist, get to know if they have successfully tackled the problem themselves. It will be more fruitful associating with someone that already has what you want. They will guide you appropriately and their methods will definitely work with you if they worked with them. You don't necessarily have to go around asking them how it is done, spending time with them is enough for you to learn their strategies over time.

If for example they normally take a nap or go for a walk when they are stressed, you will find yourself doing the same every time you feel your anxiety is about to hit the roof. Learn how that particular person has managed to forge so many healthy relationships. Follow them around whenever they are meeting new people are learn their strategies. For you to be able to get all this information, you will need to secure a spot in their circle, so it doesn't look like you are invading their personal space. Once they accept you, try to be of the best character around them. Don't be too critical and judgmental about their shortcomings as this will piss them off. Be understanding and supportive when you need to be. It will make them even more willing to share their working techniques with you. They will also help you overcome your problems in a more direct manner.

Find Yourself a Professional

Sometimes the only person that will guide you appropriately is someone that has knowledge of your condition. In the case of brain anxiety, the best person to approach is a psychotherapist. This is an option taken when the problem is almost getting out of hand. You don't necessarily have to be in a doctor-patient relationship. Once you develop a friendship with such a person, their help becomes automatic. Every time you spend with them becomes some sort of therapy session. Try to spend as much time as you can to make it productive. You can be friends with more than one professional at a go. Each one of them will teach you different and unique strategies that will come in handy. Such a coach will also help you identify people you should associate with and the ones to avoid.

One advantage of using this strategy is that you won't be gambling about the kind of person you are welcoming into your circle. It will be someone whose record is straight. Sometimes it is difficult to accurately identify a positive person you want to associate with. A unique characteristic of all professionals and experts, more so those in the medical field, is their love for honesty. Anyone can readily help you by virtue of your honesty. This is not someone that will easily judge you, so don't be afraid of opening up. If anything, your honesty will put them in a better position to help you. They will know the right buttons to press. You will be very lucky if you manage to get at least one mental disorder professional into your circle. Make that happen!

Attend counseling sessions

When you start attending counseling sessions, you don't only get to expose yourself to professional help, but you will also meet like-minded people, people that are serious about recovery and change. During such sessions, interact with those people and ask them how they are tackling their respective problems. Not down those strategies that you see have worked and apply them in your case. Ensure you open up about your own condition as this will encourage them to open up about theirs as well.

Don't forget to have a light chat with the counselor too, you will likely pick something helpful in the process. Mingling with this kind of person will enable you to create new friends that will come in handy as far as your mental anxiety is concerned. However, it is not everyone in those sessions that needs to be befriended. Chat with everyone but spend more time with people that show better signs of improvement. These are people that have a positive mind as well as better strategies. Start by congratulating them then ask how they do it. They will gladly share their secrets with you. You need these strategies to apply in your case so don't be shy about asking questions. Those that show little improvement probably have a poor attitude and strategies that are not worth copying.

Find Yourself an Understanding Partner

Your partner plays a very important role when it comes to your mental health. This is one person that you spend more time with than anyone else. The impact in your mind in a way that you might not comprehend. Technically, you become them, and they become you as the days go by. People with mental health issues have a rough time navigating relationships. Few manage to keep a healthy relationship for long. It becomes even worse if they have a partner that gives them more stress than they give support. Also, the kind of people your partner brings into your lives have an effect on your mental well-being. Maybe their family is piling pressure on both of you about certain things. This kind of pressure will likely increase your brain anxiety.

However, if your partner understands your condition, they will protect you from toxic people including their friends and relatives. Not only will your partner protect you from negative people, but they will also encourage you to find help if they can't help you themselves. This is how important it is to choose someone that is caring and compassionate for a partner. These problems might come up late when the relationship has advanced, a point where there is nothing much to live as it used to be. A good partner will stand by you whatsoever. Things get complicated when your partner starts viewing you as baggage. Your mental anxiety will get worse with such a partner, trust me.

Create a Healthy Network

Sometimes you find someone with positive energy but the kind of people they associate with are not your ideal kind of friends. Like it or not, once you let someone into your circles, you will have to accept their friends as well. This is where you get into a dilemma. You don't know whether to do away with your good friend or to ask them to do away with their 'bad' friends in order to keep your friendship. First, the second option has almost zero chance of working. The first option, on the other hand, might prove costly. So, then you have been left with only one option- create a balance for a start. Only hang around your friends when they are with their 'good' friends. You don't have to act paranoid in their presence. Do an inquiry of the people they are with before going to meet them or asking them over. If they are with those people you consider to be a bad influence, find a smart way of avoiding meeting them.

I will give you an example. Sometime, way back I used to have a very good friend whom I used to share all my issues with, and they also shared theirs with me. Unfortunately, he had this gang of guys that were always hanging out in dens drinking alcohol and smoking all kinds of illegal substances. Ironically, my friend didn't do any of that, in fact, he is a sworn teetotaler. He didn't see anything wrong with the company he kept, in fact, he would accompany them to the bar and took non-alcoholic drinks as they took theirs. This obviously upset me deeply but could not bring myself to tell him that. So, I came up with a strategy where I would ask him where he was at a certain time. If he says he is with that gang and that I could join them, I would say a bored 'no' and hang up immediately. This went on for a while until he noticed that I was not comfortable with that group. He stopped asking me to join them and whenever we bumped on each other when he is with them, he would hastily excuse himself to talk to me. That is how I managed to shield myself from that gang while at the same time maintaining a healthy friendship with my friend. This does not only happen in the case of friends, but it also applies to families. If you think that a certain family member, could be from your side or your associate's side, does not give you peace of mind, don't isolate the whole family because of that one person, keep in mind that issues with families are quite sensitive. Just make yourself unavailable to them using smart techniques. It won't take long before they realize that you are not comfortable with their behavior. This isolationist technique will help you create an almost purely healthy network of people that make you happy.

Don't be selfish with your time

Remember nothing comes easy, you have to work for it. For you to have heavy relationships with the right people, you need to be ready to invest in them. Relationships can be intimate, family, friendships or work-related. Whatever type it is, it has to be solid. The good thing about this kind of investment is that it has nothing to do with money. All you need to invest is your time. Yes, time! It is impossible to get to know someone overnight. You need patience and more time with them. They also need time to understand and appreciate you. This might not take place if you are selfish with your time, the results of which are judging and being judged wrongly. The relationship must move from step to step without trying to rush it. The stronger a relationship is, the less stressful it will be. A toxic relationship will do more harm to your brain than anything else can. Creating time happens in three stages.

Stage 1- Go where you think you can find someone with positive energy. This involves searching for social events that are being attended by people you admire. These could be parties, workshops or counseling sessions. Once you have identified where to go, do a background check on the kind of people you will be meeting. Determine whether there is a probability of you being impacted positively in that particular meeting. If you find more than one place you could visit on the same day, prioritize. Only go for the best option, don't try to attend all because you might not concentrate on your objective.

Stage 2- Having chosen where to go, make every minute count while you are in that place. Avoid engaging in idle talk whatsoever. Ask mind-provoking questions that are wired to finding a solution to your mental anxiety. Grill them like you are in an interview but with caution, get to know most things about them. Gauge their level of intellect, their ability to solve conflicts wisely and generally how they approach things. If you think the person is worth hanging around with, ask if you could see them in the future. You can take their contacts and also give yours. Try to spend as much time as possible with one person to know them. If there is still enough time at your disposal, move to the next person and the next one until it is time to leave. Be objective as you meet each one of them, remember you came looking for positive people to associate with. That should be your agenda throughout the day.

Stage 3- Having met prospective associates, sit down and analyze them keenly. Reflect on the things they had told you about themselves. Weigh each and every statement and see if it changed you in any way. Compare the experiences you had with each one of them and rank them from the best to the worst. If you think the information about or experience with a particular person is not enough to determine if you want to associate with them, look for more time to meet them again. You can make it casual or book an appointment if they have a busy schedule. Only continue associating with the people you are sure they will give you the best experience.

Chapter 12
Never Stop, Be Your Change

Throughout this book, we have established the meaning of anxiety. We have also taken a look at the sources of anxiety in general terms. We have also been keen to bring about ways of enabling individuals to face their respective fears. We have also had an overview of how to bring out optimism in our lives. We have had to practice how to keep ourselves devoid of the urge of wanting to have control over various things. Owing to this we had to look at the various techniques that help an individual maintain his or her calm whenever he or she is in situations that are demanding. We have also had an overview of a practice in which an individual is able to practice self-confidence. This was also backed by the idea of being easy on oneself especially when we commit various mistakes that make us look down upon ourselves. We have had a discussion on the inadequacies that human beings have and thus what makes us human. We have also had to appreciate our bodies in a manner that entails decoding of the various signs that the body sends when in various situations. We have also engaged in the know-how that the individuals that we keep close have a lot to say about our character as individuals.

This chapter is keen to see that an individual maintains this consistency in order to see him or her achieve whatever they desire in life. You have adopted various mechanisms that help you relax when you are tensed and the only right thing to do is to see to it that you maintain the mastery and practice of these particular techniques in order to make sure that you are ready whenever a situation arises that demands your utmost attention. The only way you will maintain consistency is by accepting that you are of dear value and thus you will direct all your attention towards making sure that you are doing what is in the best interests of yourself. There are a few things that an individual may employ in his or her everyday life in order to see to it that this type of individual operates in a manner that is advantageous to himself. The following are some pointers that when implemented, will see to it that you are consistent in the manner that you carry out yourself. Everything that separates a negative mindset from one that is positive is the idea that you can, and you are in a position that you can be able to achieve.

Know Yourself

Knowing yourself entails that you are aware of your strengths and weaknesses. This will be of aid for you in a number of ways. First, you are able to make use of your strengths. You are able to respond to your strengths in a manner that I positive towards you. This means that you will use your stents to your advantage. You will focus on engaging in the activities that you shine the best in. These types of activities are the ones that you have top-notch performance. You are excellent in the performance of such activities to the extent that you are aware of this. There are some activities that you do not need reassurance in order to know that you are the best in them. These particular types of activities are the ones that you need major your focus in order to make sure that you succeed in whatever you do.

The second type of focus will be drawn to your weaknesses. A keen look at your weaknesses will see to it that you are in a position whereby you can focus on them in order to make sure that you are improving them. One can use his or her weaknesses to their advantage in two ways. The first instance is through making sure that you improve on them and thus this can lead to turning them into your strengths. The second one entails that you refrain from engaging in activities that portray your weaknesses. This entails focusing on the situations that make that elicit your strengths and refraining from those that tend to expose you in a manner that is disadvantageous. The study has it that the discovery of an individual's advantages and disadvantages work best in ensuring that this particular type of individual succeeds in whatever input or venture. You are able to stay devoid of anxiety through the act of knowing oneself. This is because you are able to engage in activities that bring out the best in you and whatever you are doing.

Live through your fears

You have had an overview of what your fears are. You have also had to see the various techniques which may be of aid to you when conquering your fears. Now you need to have an understanding that your fears will keep on recurring and thus you will have to exercise conquering them every time that they occur. Most of the time you will find that an individual is able to overcome his or her fear the first time that they encounter it after the apt mastery of the techniques at hand. What about when the fears come without a knock on the door and you are in a position that demand s you act within a fraction of a second. This tests your ability to be able to respond when in a tight spot. Embracing your fears means that you will be able to live within your fears in a manner that suggests you are comfortable. When you achieve this, you can safely deduce that you overcame your fears.

Accept change

You have made some adjustments in your life that will see to it that there is a change in the direction that your life takes. Owing to this, you are bound to stick to those adjustments in order to make sure that the direction in which your life is headed is one that is guided. Take time and recap on how your life has been, the various mistakes that you have made. With this in mind, you will have an overview of the causes of these particular mistakes.

With this at hand, you are able to know the specific areas that you have to make adjustments that will suit your cause. For instance, if it is making adjustments in the circle you keep, you will know what kind of friends to keep and which ones you are going to cut off. Do not fall for the phobia of engaging in new activities that bring about a better you. Have an open mind to the various ideas that work as a mile mover in your life.

Own up

You have had a recap of your own life and as a result, this elicited the various mistakes that you made in your life. Do not shy away from the part that you are the perpetrator of these particular mistakes, know them and embrace them. As a result, you are in a position where you are able to focus on rebuilding yourself. Owning up requires a certain degree of acceptance that enables you to know that you have made a mistake, but you would not let it define you. This way, you are able to move from it rather than dwelling on it. The most subtle part when dealing with a mistake is when you reach a point where you have to confess to your foes and own up before them. Moreover, internal acceptance is what thrives when making someone own up. Take for instance you have been haunted by a mistake you made in the past because it keeps on manifesting itself in your brain day in day out. In order to move on from a situation like this, you need to first accord yourself some courtesy in order to have a clear vision that you have to move on and proceed with your life.

The monologue is one thing that has worked time and again. Having a conversation with yourself will see to it that you are accepting your inadequacies as not to form part of your failures but to form a solid base where you are able to rise and achieve further goals.

Embrace objectivity

In order to embrace objectivity, you will have to push yourself in order to see o that you achieve, you need to set achievable goals. This means that you will not focus on the long-term, but your focus will be directed towards the setting of short-term goals with which upon achieving, you will be able to move on and set others. When setting objectives, one ought to focus on the ones that he is in a position to achieve. For instance, an individual would set goals that he is in a position to fulfill. The setting of long-term in-achievable goals is not advisable because you are devoid of the short-term successes that act as a self-motivator towards achieving the next goal. With objectivity at hand, you are able to stay devoid of the various distractions that exist. You are in a position to chase various dreams that you have been contemplating. When objectivity is embraced, an individual is in a position whereby he or she is able to focus on self-adjustment. With this in mind, you are in a position to engage only in the activities that have merit to you. Research has shown that a set of goals right above your capabilities will see to it that you push yourself beyond your comfort zone.

Believe

You have had an overview of the various technologies that an individual may employ when conquering one's fears. We have seen the various issues that make one move from a situation where he is in a state of anxiety to a state that suggests differently. The belief that the various techniques will work when employed is the first step towards making sure that you achieve. The sense of belief is one that is inborn and thus it is not derived from anywhere else. With belief, this works as self-acceptance that the process you are engaging in will work for you. Belief works like a hope that the situation at hand will change for the better and not for the worst. Accepting the techniques as forming part of you and thus going through sheer perseverance in order to achieve is one step towards making yourself a better person. Most individuals succeed in whatever they take part in because of the perception that they accord a particular sense. The belief placed in the process is what will aid you when you are on the verge of wanting to achieve.

Inquire

The inquiry is considered as being one step away from the solution. When you are encountered with various issues that you are not in a position to settle, you ought not to let that issue burn you from the inside, you can simply let it go by inquiry or sharing. One of the popular methods of acquisition of wisdom is through inquiry. An individual who goes a notch higher into inquiry sees to it he or she arrives at the solution in which he or she was seeking. In some cases, you find that an individual who has the ability to make an inquiry is often the one who accrues a lot of information. With inquiry, you are able to unearth the various novel techniques that you can use in a bid to counter anxiety. With this at hand, you are in a position where you can easily do away with anxiety once and for all.

Embrace time consciousness

How you manage your time has a big implication on the various activities that you are able to engage in. Time management is key in the sense that this is a scarce resource that we all accrue equality to. Every individual inconsiderate of the social class has a maximum of twenty-four hours a day and how you use this particular time will see to it that you maximize on the various goals that we have set in mind. Time is of the essence and you need to put into consideration time-consciousness if at all you want to achieve in any particular field. Look at the various causes of anxiety, your brain releases specific neurons when you are anxious, these particular neurons work in order to affect the various feelings that one has in his or her mind. When you are conscious about your time, you are particularly engaged to the extent that anxiety would not form any distraction to you. When you are conscious about your time, you find that achieving what you have set becomes less subtle. Take for instance you have various anxiety issues when it comes to different issues. Often you may be involved in various issues that make you anxious but because you are too busy, you may fail to notice them.

Intensify

Intensity comes in as a positive factor. Any people are in their comfort zones and as a result of this, such people do not make the most out of themselves. This is because they do not push themselves beyond the limits of living. Living with intensity entails that you push yourself beyond the limits that exist. Sometimes, individuals tend to set limits in their brains. An individual will be inclined to visualize himself as being inferior and not in a position to be able to achieve. When this happens, an individual cannot function past the limits of a particular state. Most of the time you will find that individuals are carried away by thoughts of inferiority to the extent that they fail to participate in various activities that they fully have the capacity to do so. When engaging in a particular activity, it is of key importance that an individual focuses his or her efforts towards achieving.

Exercising Integrity

Exercising integrity refers to staying stern in whatever decision that you take. The act of integrity refers to sticking to what is right no matter the situation. Loyalty and integrity go hand in hand in the sense that they are inborn feelings. You cannot ask it from someone else you can only demand it from yourself. With integrity, you are in a position whereby you are able to focus on the right things in life. This means that you are not in putting yourself in situations whereby an individual will doubt you. Most people who exercise integrity have found themselves on the verge of many important positions. This is because this particular type of person will be able to act in the right manner when it is required of him. Most of the time people fail to understand that staying true to the rightful cause is what will ensure that you rise to the top. As a result of this, you find that this particular type of individual is in a position to act in a manner that suggests cheekiness which will, in turn, lead to the individual not getting to where he or she wants. The result is always a failure that cannot be reversed. It is important to practice integrity because this is a virtue. When you are full of integrity, most likely the doors will open for you and you will stay devoid of anxiety. This is because you are able to make choices that influence positively on your resume' and you would not have time to worry.

Welcome Criticism

A lot of people are affected by criticism due to the negative energy that comes with it. Criticism is always the hardest of words to decode but often the truth. The veracity of these words is what makes it subtle for an individual to face them. When an individual is criticized, they are in a position to either channel this critic towards the positive side outwards the negative side. When an individual is criticized and as a result, he or she channels the critic to the negative, this is often the direction that most individuals take. You will find that this individual is in a position to look down upon himself or herself. When this happens, this individual uses this as a reference point of not engaging in further activities. You will find that the whole life of an individual is based on some particular facts that put him or her down once. When the energy is directed positively, you find that this particular individual is able to learn from his or her past mistakes and as a result, advance from these particular mistakes. When this happens, the individual is able to better themselves. When you welcome criticism, you are in a position not to be affected by the anxiety that comes with various phobias.

Live Rightfully

Living rightfully is a topic that circumvents various topics. The life of a particular individual is composed of various aspects that work in a bid to make it worth living. An individual who does not put into consideration various factors will see to it that he or she faces challenges at some point in their lives. So, consider the aspect of feeding healthy, people tend to ignore this particular face of life until they are encountered with diseases that demand reconsideration and outlook on the foods that a particular individual ingests. When we live rightfully, we are in a position to make sure that we maintain a balanced diet that is required in order to lead healthy lives. Living rightfully can also be attributed to the various actions that we engage in. For instance, an individual who engages in the right activities in life will often find himself or herself achieving the right results in life. Living rightfully although ignored, is a fact that tends to impact a lot in our lives.

Conclusions

Thank you for making it to the end of this book. If you are reading this, it is because you are keen on improving your overall wellbeing. In addition, you are making considerable strides in dealing with those aspects which have been affecting your life in a negative manner.

So, the next step now is to focus on improving your mindset so that you set yourself up for success. The fact of the matter is that you are your own enemy when you either deliberately, or unconsciously, sabotage yourself. You can set yourself up for success by making the necessary mental adjustments that will lead you to become a force to be reckoned with.

Please take the time to go over the exercises that we have outlined in this book. These exercises will provide you with the boost you need to help you get over those issues which are holding you back. Moreover, you will find that making the most of your talents is not only essential to your success, but also vital to making the world around you a better place.

Doesn't that sound like something?

You have the power to make the world around you a better place by being keen on improving the lives of others. Now, you don't need to make world-altering changes; all you need is to put your best foot forward and the rest will fall into place. You will be able to make the most of your opportunities to make everyone feel better about themselves and about their lives.

Thanks again for taking the time to read this book. If you have found it to be useful and informative, then do please tell your friends and family about it. Surely, they will find the same usefulness in it as you have.

See you in the next installment!

Made in the USA
Monee, IL
10 January 2023

24962707R00079